THE REVELATIONS
OF ADELHEID LANGMANN

The Revelations of Adelheid Langmann

Introduced and translated by
LEONARD P. HINDSLEY

LUMINARE PRESS
WWW.LUMINAREPRESS.COM

The Revelations of Adelheid Langmann
Copyright © 2021 by Leonard P. Hindsley

Revised Edition © 2024

All rights reserved. This book or any portion thereof may not be reproduced or used in any manner whatsoever without the express written permission of the publisher, except for the use of brief quotations in a book review.

Printed in the United States of America

Luminare Press
442 Charnelton St.
Eugene, OR 97401
www.luminarepress.com

LCCN: 2024904314
ISBN: 979-8-88679-515-8

For Sr. Mary Paul of Christ
and the nuns of St. Dominic Monastery
Linden, Virginia

*Ecce quam bonum et quam jucundum
habitare sorores in unum*

Contents

Preface . . . . *ix*
Preface to the Second Edition . . . . *xii*
Acknowledgments . . . . *xiii*
Introduction 1

Part One: Context

CHAPTER ONE
Adelheid Langmann and the Monastery of Engelthal 7

CHAPTER TWO
Dominican Monasticism 21

CHAPTER THREE
Scriptural Influences 49

CHAPTER FOUR
Literary Sources 61

CHAPTER FIVE
Manuscripts and Texts 81

Part Two: Texts

The *Revelations* of Adelheid Langmann 97

The *Prayer* of Adelheid Langmann 160

Excerpts of Correspondence 171

Select Bibliography 177
Author Biography 183
Endnotes 185
Index to Texts 205

Preface

With the publication of this book the life and works of a previously obscure German mystic come to light in the English-speaking world. The literary works of women, such as Adelheid Langmann, suffered the fate of obscurity for historical, theological and linguistic reasons. Adelheid, like others, chose to record her autobiographical *Revelations* in her native German tongue rather than in ecclesiastical Latin. This limited her audience in her own time to her own circle of spiritually like-minded individuals who formed a large, but relatively closed group of fervent Christians. The rapid development of the German language over the next hundred years made it difficult for her writings to be understood by later generations. Theologically, Adelheid belonged to a group called the Friends of God, who in retrospect were sometimes confused with a later heterodox group by the same name, and therefore little incentive existed to translate these writings into Latin or to update them in German. Later ages and theologies, less in touch with the mystic dimension of religion, found no reason to perpetuate and celebrate the experiences and writings of fourteenth-century women. Historically, the writings of Adelheid and of most of her generation at the Monastery of Engelthal suffered theological banishment because of the Protestant Reformation. Nuremberg was the first Free Imperial City to accept and impose the teachings of the Reformation. The City Counsillors zealously broke with the old religion and began to suspect the religious sentiments of earlier times. Among the nuns of Engelthal only the memory of Christina

Ebner endured due to the prominence of her family. The Ebner von Eschenbach family made certain that her works were copied and preserved. They even erected a shrine to her above a door in the parish church of St. Sebaldus in Nuremberg—a carved group consisting of the Virgin and Child with Christina as a Dominican nun kneeling at their feet. Below this group a succession of Ebners was painted memorializing the family.

This book contains a critical translation into English of Adelheid Langmann's *Revelations*, her *Prayer*, and correspondence. As well as these primary texts the book provides commentary and interpretation of Adelheid Langmann's *Revelations*. It should draw a wide readership of scholars from the fields of women's studies, theology, spirituality, social history, German medieval studies and Dominican studies. For women's studies, the autobiography of a hitherto unknown figure prominent in her own time would prove invaluable as a document of revelation into the life, thought and concerns of a woman during a particularly exciting century of spiritual expression. Theologians would find in the texts a case study in practical, mystical theology and in the theological reflections of a woman given to deeper insight. Along with scholars of spirituality, they would wish to learn what theological figures such as Mechthild of Magdeburg, Thomas Aquinas, Bernard of Clairvaux and German mystics influenced the thought of Adelheid Langmann. They would be intrigued by her practically unique (among her contemporaries) emphasis on a Trinitarian spirituality marked by vivid images of Divine Indwelling. Social historians would find a rich documentary of life in a fourteenth-century monastery from the perspective of one individual and have a glimpse through her eyes of the inner workings of a cloistered community. These texts would prove helpful to students of German medieval studies for many of the same reasons. For Dominican studies, the writings of Adelheid Langmann, reveal the lived experience of members of the Order of Preachers during the greatest flowering of Dominican spirituality and mysticism and shows the impact of the theological themes and beliefs as preached and taught, here as received and lived. Chapters One through Five of this volume are based on parts of Chapters One, Four, Seven and Eight of my book *The Mystics of Engelthal: Writings from a Medieval Monastery* (St. Martin's Press, 1998). However, the material that appears in *The Revelations of Adelheid Langman* has been extensively reworked, augmented and revised.

Preface to the Second Edition

When I received the hard copy of the first edition of *The Revelations of Adelheid Langmann* I was chagrined to see that the book did not come out as planned. I complained to KDP and was told to engage professional help. So here is the second edition, much, much improved. I apologize to all those who purchased the first edition. The content was great and useful, but the format and design left much to be desired. I thank Patricia Marschall, the owner and editor of Luminare Press for her guidance and encouragement. Thanks also to Kim Harper-Kennedy, project and operations manager and my main contact throughout the editing and publishing process. Caitlin McCrum, publication assistant, helped a great deal with the final stages of the whole process. Many thanks to Kristen Brack, graphic designer for the cover design. Thank you very much to the entire team at Luminare Press. They produce books that are readable as well as beautiful.

Acknowledgments

I wish to thank Fr. Josef Zborzil and the Dominican community of St. Albert the Great parish in Munich for their kindness and hospitality during my sabbatical studies and research. Also, thanks to the priors and members of the Dominican communities in Berlin, Vienna and London who offered me hospitality while researching manuscripts in those cities. Thank you to Adelheid Toussignant, who offered assistance in checking the translation at one stage of the process. For her careful reading of the manuscript and insightful suggestions for improvement I thank Professor Ann-Maria Contarino. I am grateful to others who have offered assistance and support to me while I wrote this book: Fr. Nicholas Ingham, Fr. Iriarte Andujar, and especially Alex Naglowsky without whose help this book would never have made it to print. Many thanks to Paula Brown for her invaluable support and help with technical difficulties in preparing the manuscript to be published. Without these helpers and friends it would have been impossible to bring out this book. *Vergelt's Gott!* For this second edition I offer thanks to the editorial team at Luminare Press, who refashioned the first edition into a text that is both easily readable and lovely.

Introduction

The death of Sister Adelheid Langmann on 22 November 1375 marked the end of the intense mystical life recorded by the nuns at the monastery of Engelthal in Bavaria. Previously Sister Christina Ebner (1277-1356), had recorded the remarkable lives and mystical experiences of the nuns. chaplains and brothers at the community at Engelthal from before the founding of the monastery in 1244 to the flowering of mystical culture during the fourteenth century in the *Sister-Book* (*Schwesternbuch*) of the monastery. In the fourteenth century the monastery of Engelthal held the pre-eminent position in Dominican mysticism. No other Dominican foundation of nuns produced such a volume and variety of mystical works among which the *Revelations* of Adelheid Langmann takes an important place.

This book presents a complete translation into English from the Middle High German texts of Adelheid Langmann, including her autobiographical *Revelations*, her *Prayer*, and her correspondence with Ulrich Niblung, a Cistercian monk of the nearby Cistercian Monastery of Kaisheim. This translation with background and contextual information adds to the necessary research and publication required for a fuller study of a distinctive mysticism of Engelthal. None of the works in the body of Engelthal literature has been translated into English, except for my recently published *The Sister-Book of Engelthal*. *The Life of Gertrud of Engelthal* and the *Life of Grace of Friedrich Sunder* have appeared only in Middle High German. Christina Ebner's *Sister-Book of Engelthal* has been published in Middle High German and in modern German translations, but her *Revelations* exist only in the various late medieval manuscripts housed in Stuttgart, Nuremberg and Medingen. Karl Schröder published the Middle High German text of the *Sister-Book of Engelthal* under the title *Der Nonne von Engelthal Büchlein von der Gnaden Überlast* in 1871. Margarethe Weinhandl published a translation of that text in 1921. Working independently Wilhelm Oehl also brought out a translation in 1924. Only brief excerpts of Christina Ebner's *Revelations* had been translated earlier in 1872 by G.W.K. Lochner. More primary work is required to begin a comprehensive description of the spirituality of the Dominicans of Engelthal. This translation contributes to that study of the mysticism of the nuns of Englalthal by making a complete English translation of Adelheid Langmann's autobiographical *Revelations* available. Then other scholars may begin to write about the distinctive contribution to theology, spirituality and to women's studies made by Adelheid Langmann and her religious sisters and associates at Engelthal.

Part One of this book contains sections on various topics necessary to understand Adelheid Langmann and her writings within the context of her times according to the cultural, political and religious influences exerted upon her and which found expression in her *Revelations*. Because Adelheid Langmann was a Dominican nun, I have included a treatment of Dominican monasticism in order to connect the documentary basis of the practical living out of that distinctive form of monasticism with the spirit of St. Dominic which the Constitutions, as revised by Humbert of Romans, expressed. I discuss the context of the Dominican monastic milieu: the structure and plan of the monastery building itself, the daily horarium of prayer and work and the role of study, since a precise knowledge of the elements of monastic observance can not be assumed of the modern reader. The rules contained in the Constitutions and the interplay among the elements of daily life form the basis for interpreting monastic life as predisposing mystical life.

Scholars have argued that the causes for this flowering of mystical life in fourteenth-century Dominican monasteries had to do with social, political and climactic conditions. Certainly the assertion that causes such as floods, earthquakes, plagues, political strife, schism and interdict have exerted in contributing to a certain otherworldly *Weltanschauung* in the fourteenth century have merit. These serve as contributing factors, but are certainly not the causes of the flourishing of mysticism in the fourteenth century. The ideal of mystical life sprang from the belief of the nuns that the Triune God invited them to experience ecstatic mystical life which traversed the boundaries of time and space inviting the nun to respond to the intimacies of Christ, to befriend the Virgin Mary and other saints, to intercede powerfully for the souls in purgatory and to counsel those who sought the advice and guidance of the nuns in spiritual matters on earth.

The history of the monastery of Engelthal is the concrete setting for this flowering of mysticism. It shows the development of a group of Christian women from Nuremberg who formed themselves first into a band of beguines and then eventually, having discerned the need to adopt a more monastic mode of life, into the vocation of nuns in association with the fledgling Dominican Order. Its history situates this "garden" of mysticism within the context of the temporal and spiritual struggles of the age. The nuns were caught in the power struggles of the patrician and noble families that claimed benefits, in particular, from their monastic lands and revenues. In spite of the the interdict and the general confusion over papal authority and imperial power, the nuns forthrightly professed their faith in Jesus Christ in a time that sorely tested the faith of all Christians.

The *Revelations* and external sources present a picture of Adelheid Langmann as a particularly pious girl from the patrician burgher class of the powerful city of Nuremberg. She chose to accept a monastic vocation, in spite of the opposition of herself and her family. Having accepted the vocation of a nun, Adelheid flourished spiritually and practically under the cloistral regimen. She acquired an education from the nuns and demonstrated both knowledge of Latin and the ability to read and write in her native German. Adelheid's learning, acquired through study and the normal readings in the cloister, as well as from the preaching she heard, and the exchange of information in letters, shows knowledge of biblical texts, especially the *Song of Songs*, The *Book of Revelation* and the letters of St. Paul. She made use of translations and commentaries such as the *St. Trutperter Song of Songs* and the sermons *On the Song of Songs* by Bernard of Clairvaux. Mechthild of Magdeburg's *The Flowing Light of the Godhead*, among other mystical texts, certainly exerted an influence on her thought, her imaginative worldview and writings.

Finally, I analyze the three extant manuscripts of Adelheid Langmann's *Revelations*, noting their similarities and differences. The introductory chapters serve to put the present translation into the context of its society, culture and religious situation.

I have divided the translation of the German text into paragraphs corresponding to the divisions in the manuscripts. Each paragraph is numbered for reference purposes since the three manuscripts do not agree on the placement or sequence of paragraphs.

PART ONE

Context

CHAPTER ONE

Adelheid Langmann and the Monastery of Engelthal

Adelheid Langmann's autobiographical book called *Revelations,* provides firsthand information about her life before entering the monastery as well as her years as a nun. Further information exists in public documents such as deeds, the records of the city of Nuremberg and the account books of the monastery to help fill out information on her life. Information from these documents adds background detail to what is stated in the *Revelations*. They also clarify the social status of her family and reveal the rich tapestry of connections interwoven by the monastic community and the families of the nuns. Each nun's life was inextricably united with the life of the community whose history, ethos and ideals in turn impacted the lives and spirituality of the nuns individually and collectively. The monastery, the families of the nuns, the city authorities and the people of Nuremberg formed an extended social unit which depended upon all three parts. Not surprisingly the nuns' families proudly identified themselves first as citizens of the free imperial city and secondarily as devotees of the monastery at Engelthal. This interest of these families depended upon the fact that a daughter or sister had become a nun at Engelthal. When a woman decided to enter into the religious community, it was customary for her family to provide a dowry of land with revenues that would be used for the support of the monastery, corresponding to the land and revenues that would have been her dowry for marriage. This was the expected offering from the families whose daughters became choir sisters. As with other monasteries the admission of a new nun was restricted according to her status in the world. Some monasteries were royal foundations—admission being reserved to women of royal birth. The monastery of Engelthal admitted as choir nuns daughters of the noble classes which included not only landed nobility and gentry, but patrician families from the city and families of the imperial or royal ministerial classes. Even though the nuns had distanced themselves from their families at a monastery located far outside the city, familial and civil bonds remained strong, so strong in fact that one day they would bring the monastery to its end.

The Life of Adelheid Langmann

Adelheid Langmann's book entitled *Revelations* serves as the major source of information with regard to her inner life, thought and mystical experiences. From this text and from external sources it is known that Adelheid was born into a patrician family of Nuremberg around 1312 A.D. The exact date of birth was not given in the Berlin (B) manuscript of the *Revelations*, however it states clearly there that she was born in Nuremberg. At the tender age of thirteen her family engaged her to a young man named Gottfried Teufel, who soon died (2). It seems that the marriage was never consummated. Although many had thought she belonged in a monastery, Adelheid Langmann resisted this idea. After a struggle with her own unwillingness to accept a monastic vocation, and with the disapproval of her family members who wanted her to marry, she eventually entered the Monastery of Engelthal between 1327 and 1330. Adelheid consented to become a nun only after she had accepted the call according to Christ's will expressed in visions, and with the affirmation of other spiritual people.

In the *Revelations* Adelheid Langmann recorded the events of her life from 1330 to 1344, recalling memories from her childhood, and reporting revelations received about the future. Among the more important events she related the following should be noted. On the eve of her profession of vows Adelheid Langmann experienced diabolic temptations meant to prevent her from becoming a nun (88). On All Saints Day she descended into purgatory and found out that many people (including her mother), whom everyone thought had already attained heavenly bliss, were still awaiting deliverance from purgatory although they no longer suffered in any way except for the lack of the vision of God (91). She prayed earnestly for a perfect conformity of her will with the will of Christ. She enjoyed an ever progressive intimacy with her Beloved—Jesus Christ—as noted by various incidents such as the inscription of Christ's name upon her heart and her name upon his (15, 25, 32, 117), a kind of exchange of hearts also experienced by other mystics such as Margaret Ebner. According to Siegfried Ringler the apex of this progression of mystical espousals occurred in the episode where *Caritas* and *Spes,* personifications of Love and Hope, led her to the bed of love where mystical union took place.[1]

> The Lord now approached the bed. In all his joyous beauty he knelt down before the bed and his face was turned toward mine. I looked up and gazed at him. He was so beautiful that I could not bear it and it seemed to me that my soul would dissolve from true love. He said, "My Beloved!" With the same word that so sweetly came out from his mouth he drew my poor, sinful soul into his Godhead and I can say nothing about this vision . . . (72).

The significance of this passage rests not only on its content, but on the sudden shift in person in the relation of the account. Rarely did Adelheid Langmann write her narrative in the first person. She typically distanced herself from the narrative by referring to herself impersonally as a "sister" or by using the third person pronoun. It seems that the ecstatic exultation in remembering this event compelled her to personalize the account by using the first person pronoun, perhaps because the experience was and remained so powerful to her even as she wrote about it in retrospect.

Gustav Voit showed that documentary evidence dated 8 August 1327 states that Adelheid was the widow of Gottfried Teufel and that she had received an estate at Happurg from her mother, Mechthild Langmann, a resident of Nuremberg and the widow of Otto Langmann. Other documents show that on 20 June 1339, Adelheid Langmann purchased an estate at Traunfeld from Henry II Steinlinger from Lauterhofen.[2] In 1350 she received revenues from a house in Offenhausen, from estates at Ittelshofen, Schmiede, Traunfeld, Happurg, Speikern and a share in the revenues from another estate in Traunfeld.[3] After Adelheid's death revenues from Offenhausen were to be donated to the monastery to observe the anniversary of the death of Adelheid's mother, Mechthild. The rents from Ittelshofen would go toward the observance of the anniversary of the death of Sr. Kunigunde Forchheimer. Also after her death the rents from Happurg and Speikern would fall to her nieces, Gerhaus and Margarete Sachsen, both nuns of Engelthal.

Adelheid began to write her *Revelations* around 1330 at the request of an unnamed, but prominent Dominican priest and was probably still writing in 1350.[4] She lived uninterruptedly within the monastic enclosure until she died on 22 November 1375.

In her *Revelations* Adelheid noted that she had relatives in the monastery (71) and stated that her aunt had received an office in the monastery (46). Sophia Langmann, her sister, also lived as a nun at Engelthal as did two of her nieces—Gerhaus and Margarete Sachsen. Adelheid was probably also related to Elsbet Mayer (her goddaughter) and to Gerhaus Mayer with whom she shared revenues from an estate at Traunfeld.[5] Kunigunde Forchheimer and Elisabeth of Eyb may also have been related as well since both nuns and their families were commemorated by the monastery at the same time. There is a possibility of a relation to the Engelthal nun Christina Ebner, since Friedrich Ebner's daughter Agnes married Hermann Langmann on 14 June 1344. Also, the second wife of a Herman Ebner who died in 1403, was Kunigunde Langmann.[6] The Berlin manuscript (B) claimed that the Ebners and the Langmanns were related. Finally, it is evident that the Church of St. Sebaldus in Nuremberg was the parish church of both the Ebner and the Langmann families. Their coats-of-arms are displayed side-by-side in one of the stained glass windows of the church.

The Chronicles of the city of Nuremberg also record a coat-of-arms for the Langmann family (which matches the arms displayed in St. Sebaldus church) and a brief history of the Langmanns.[7] Although they seem never to have been numerous, they held positions of responsibility in the city.[8] Hans Langmann became a city councillor in 1349 and died in 1371. Otto Langmann likewise served as a city councillor until 1370 and then hanged himself in his bedroom on 31 August 1375.[9] This Otto and Hans were likely Adelheid's brothers. From external sources it is known that Adelheid's brothers were named Hans and Otto and her sister Jutta (Geut) married Henry of Sachsen, while another sister, Sophia, also became a nun of Engelthal.[10] In Martini's *Historisch-geographische Beschreibung des ehemaligen berühmten Frauenklosters Engeltal* (1798), he referred to "herr Conrad Langmann" (1318), and to "Mechtild Langmann from Nuremberg, nun at Engelthal" (1338).[11] He also showed that a vigil and a Mass were recited during the week following the feast of St. Michael (29 September) for Adelheid Langmann and her family, for Sister Elisabeth of Eyb and her family, Geut Sechsin (Sachsen), and for Kunigunde Forchheimer.[12] A vigil and a Mass were also recited for Adelheid Langmann and her family during Holy Week.[13]

Adelheid Langmann, even though a cloistered nun, became widely known due to her mystical experiences and powerful intercession. Her reputation caused many, even total strangers, to seek her out asking for her advice and prayerful intercession. Men such as Marquard Tockler (61), Eckhart of Hohenstein (70) and Eberhard

Schutz (71) sought her counsel and ultimately followed her advice. However, Adelheid's widowed aunt refused to accept her advice to enter the monastery, took another husband instead and soon suffered the predicted consequences: illness and death (90).

The prominent status of the Langmann family as leaders in a free imperial city, as well as their attachment to the parish church made a life-long impression on Adelheid. The parish church of St. Sebaldus played a crucial role in forming Adelheid's religious worldview. She related that she paid careful attention to the sermons in church and pondered their meaning when she went home (1). Such a precocious child would not have failed to notice the art work and decoration of the church meant to preach the Gospel to the illiterate and to glorify God. When one considers the subsequent spiritual experiences and teachings of Adelheid it is not surprising to find their basis displayed in the stone carvings around the church. On entering the church one had to pass by a scene of angels rescuing souls from purgatory. This image, along with the Judgment scene above the entrance could well have impressed the religious imagination of the child at an early age. It would not be surprising to recall that Adelheid became a nun of the monastery of the angels (Engelthal) rather than the Dominican monastery of St. Katharine founded in 1295 located within the city walls of Nuremberg. In the monastery she devoted herself especially to praying for the release of souls from purgatory. Adelheid Langmann also wrote about the events of the Last Day on which Christ comes in glory to judge the living and the dead. The Trinity is prominently displayed in the carvings around the parish church. Her spirituality is emphatically Trinitarian rather than Christocentric, which would be the norm for her contemporaries. The image of the Virgin Mary spreading her wide mantle of protection over the people also appears both in the stone carvings of the church of St. Sebaldus and in the imagery Adelheid uses in the *Revelations*.

Adelheid seems to have been predisposed to join the monastery of Engelthal by her family connections and by her imaginative religious worldview which led her to identify with the angels, who worship before the Triune God, do his will and intercede for others before his throne. She also associated herself with the Order of Preachers for she loved to hear the preaching. Her entrance into the Dominican monastery also placed her under the spiritual influence of its unique history.

The History of the Community of Engelthal

On 9 June 1244 with the election of Diemut of Gailenhausen as prioress, the history of the monastery of Engelthal as a Dominican foundation began.[14] It should be noted that its history as a religious house began some years earlier when a group of women were inspired by and gathered around Adelheid Rotter, to become beguines living in the city of Nuremberg. Like so many others in the thirteenth century, they were greatly inspired by the new ideal of imitating Christ in poverty in order to be free to serve others and to inspire them to charity. Adelheid Rotter had been previously in royal service and had accompanied the Princess Elizabeth (1207-1231), daughter of King Andrew II of Hungary to Thuringia in 1211 to be engaged to Louis IV, landgrave of Hesse and Thuringia. Later Adelheid gave up her "sinful life" and became a penitent in Nuremberg living as a beguine. As was often the case, groups of beguines would gradually commit themselves to a deeper and more organized form of religious life, realizing that the beguinage did not really meet their own spiritual needs. Many decided to become associated with the Cistercian Order or other monastic foundations. However the majority of such beguines chose to accept the way of life of the nuns of the Dominican Order. The change in Adelheid Rotter's group of followers began when they left the free imperial city of Nuremberg because Emperor Frederick II had been placed under interdict and excommunication on 11 April 1240 by Pope Gregory IX.[15] A nobleman, Ulrich II of Königstein offered the beguines protection and assistance by permitting the community to stay on his dairy farm at Engelschalksdorf near Swinach. According to Christina Ebner in her *Sister-Book* of the monastery written still within the memory of the first nuns, the women struggled for survival on the dairy farm. "There God tried them as gold is tested in fire. They had to work hard and had to cut the corn themselves and wash and bake and do all the daily chores. They did this with reverence and patience. They built a chapel in honor of St. Lawrence."[16] Despite these domestic hardships, these women also cared for the sick and the poor of the surrounding area.[17] Some time between 6 October 1241 and Easter 1243, the women nursed Ulrich III of Königstein, the grandson of their patron, Ulrich II. The boy had fallen from his horse near to Engelschalksdorf and had been taken to them for care. However he died, and with the boy's death all hope of a Königstein heir perished as well, since his father, Werntz II of Königstein, had predeceased him. As Christina Ebner reported in the *Sisterbook of Engelthal*: "That made him (Ulrich II) very sad because he had no heir other than a daughter."[18] In mourning, Ulrich II often visited the women and despite the fact that he could neither read nor write, sang along with them as they chanted the divine office.[19] After Easter 1243, Ulrich II of Königstein decided to leave his entire estate at Swinach to the beguines and stipulated that during his lifetime they would receive the revenues from the property. His wife, Adelheid, and his daughter Elizabeth were in agreement with his wishes. His son-in-law, Walter of Klingenburg, witnessed the document.[20] The soon-to-be nuns were expected to pray *in perpetuum* for the souls of the founder, his ancestors and descendants. The monastery would also provide a suitable place of burial for family members. As a result of this gift Ulrich expected the nuns to accept women of the nobility into the community and to establish a working scriptorium for all manner of correspondence.[21]

The creation of a new monastic foundation seemed feasible at that time. The Cistercians tried to convince the community of women to associate themselves with their Order. However the Cistercians did not succeed perhaps because the religious inclination and sentiment of these future Dominicans led them in the direction of the newly founded mendicant order. Because the nuns began to call their house "Engelthal" (Valley of the angels) Voit asserted that they already had an inclination to become Dominicans who sometimes named their monasteries in a similar way (Klingenthal, Wonnenthal, Engelthal in the Black Forest, Löwental).[22] In any case the association of a monastery with angels (Engelthal) must have seemed more appropriate than with swine (Swinach). Christina Ebner gave some credit for the change in name to Ulrich II.[23] However that may be, the fact remains that Bishop Frederick II of Eichstätt granted the request of Adelheid Rotter and her seven companions to establish a monastery at Engelthal according to the Rule of St. Augustine and the statutes of the Sisters of San Sisto in Rome.[24] This Statutes of San Sisto originated with Saint Dominic himself when he founded the first monastery of Dominican nuns in southern France at Prouille in 1206/7. That Rule was later used by him to gather a reform foundation of nuns at the monastery of San Sisto in Rome. By associating their monastery with the Order of Friars Preachers (Dominicans) the new nuns of Engelthal had the right of spiritual care from the preachers and initially placed themselves under the *cura animarum* of the Dominicans friars at Regensburg.[25]

A papal bull dated 4 April 1246 redefined the relationship of Dominican nuns and friars.[26] Henceforth all monasteries of nuns would come directly under the care of the Master of the Dominican Order in Rome and the Prior Provincial of the province in which the monastery was located. The Prior Provincial was required by statute to make an annual visitation and to assign educated preachers to care for the spiritual needs of the nuns. However, Dominican friars were neither required nor encouraged to reside at a monastery of nuns and thus the daily spiritual ministrations had to be met by a secular chaplain.[27] Also, the friars, chaplains and bishop played no role In the inner life and administration of the nuns in their monastery, leaving the sisters to govern themselves independent of any outside authority ecclesiastical or secular. The sisters who professed vows longer than twelve years had the right and obligation to elect the prioress, their superior, for a set term of office. Only then did the bishop or the provincial confirm the election. To be eligible for election as prioress a sister had to be at least thirty years old. She herself chose her own sub-prioress and councillors.

After the decision to become Dominican nuns and the election of the first prioress, Diemut of Gailenhausen, a delegation consisting of the prioress, a sister companion, and a lay brother made the arduous journey to Lyon to petition Pope Innocent IV to grant papal approval for the incorporation of the monastery at Engelthal into the Dominican Order. Christina Ebner states that they found a sponsor at the papal court who helped them with the petition. "There was a brother . . . who perceived their serious intention and their holiness and made known their desires to the Pope . . . and the Pope confirmed their privileges with a letter."[28] Voit suggested this may have been Cardinal Hugo of St. Cher, who was known to have sponsored many monasteries in just such a request.[29] Whoever their advocate may have been, Innocent IV signed a letter on 20 September 1248 placing the prioress and monastery "de Swina et Engeldal . . . of the Order of St. Augustine" under the care of the Master of the Order of Friars Preachers and also of the Prior Provincial of Germany.[30] Unlike the mendicant friars, the nuns of the Order could own property for their living and sustenance. A further papal letter was procured by the prioress, Diemut, on 10 October 1248, which not only guaranteed their properties, but freed the nuns from any interference from the noble families who had supported them. These benefactors could make no claim on rents and revenues from the lands they had previously donated or offered as dowry to the monastery. Over time this would set the stage for numerous disputes between the monastery and its benefactors whose daughters were nuns of Engelthal. The well intentioned directives of a distant pope often proved ineffective in protecting the rights and claims of the nuns throughout the course of the history of Engelthal especially when the powerful Schenk family in its various branches made claims upon the revenues of the monastic holdings. These heirs of Ulrich II, the founder of Engelthal, had among their family members the local bishop, and at least seven nuns of Engelthal—Ursula Schenk of Geyern, Elsbet Schenk of Klingenburg, Anna, Elsbet, another Elsbet, Katharina and Maria Schenk of Reicheneck, three of whom held the office of prioress a total of six times.[31] With so many Schenk sisters, the family must have given a great deal of land to the monastery. Despite the papal bull frequently the Schenks and other powerful families continued to exact revenues from lands donated to the monastery. The conflict with the Schenk of Reicheneck family may well have been the reason for the possibility of flight from the monastery that Adelheid Langmann recorded in her *Revelations*. "The danger was so great because the nuns were threatened that the monastery would be set afire and the animals would be taken."[32] As Adelheid reported, the prioress wished to flee from the conflict. Fortunately the violent threats were never carried out and the nuns remained safely in their monastery. Ironically, the last of the Schenk of Reichenecks died in 1458, a nun of Engelthal.[33]

The surviving monastic buildings date from the second half of the thirteenth century and are still used today, having been rebuilt following a fire in the sixteenth century. The remnants of the former monastic enclosure are located across from the former chapel of St. Willibald consecrated between 1057 and 1060.[34] Although the *Sister-Book* mentioned a chapel dedicated to St. Lawrence, the monastic church was dedicated in 1265 to St. John the Baptist. The monastery consisted of two cloisters—one for the monastery of the nuns connected to the chapel and another cloister for the buildings needed for work on the farm and for the maintenance of the complex. Around the entire monastery the nuns had a wall built with three towered gates of which two remain. Over the years the monastery received gifts of land and dowries from the wealthy families whose daughters had become nuns. Recorded in the first account book of the monastery in 1312 are one-hundred-seventy-five properties in fifty-four locations. By 1350 there were seventy more farms, estates etc. By the end of the thirteenth century the monastery possessed almost the entire valley of Hammerbach.[35]

The apex of the monastery's political history was the visit of the king of Bohemia, later Emperor Charles IV (1316-1378) on 28 May 1350.[36] The king came to visit Christina Ebner, not Adelheid Langmann. "On the same day the Roman King, a bishop, three dukes and many counts came and knelt down before her greatly desiring that she give them something to drink and a blessing."[37] Likewise Johann II, Burggraf of Nuremberg also came to visit Christina that same year.[38] Other important figures such as Henry of Nördlingen, the spiritual father, friend and later follower of Margaret Ebner, also came to visit Christina Ebner in 1351 and introduced Christina to the teachings of Suso and Tauler.[39]

Engelthal was the foremost center of mystical life among the nuns of Germany, if not all of Europe, in the fourteenth century. The visits of spiritual and great persons shows the nuns were held in high regard. More importantly, its reputation drew many young women to take the veil as nuns at Engelthal. It may well be that over one-hundred nuns and lay sisters led the religious life within the cloistered walls of the monastery. The sisters grew in number to such an extent that it became necessary to found a daughter house. In 1269, Sr. Mechthild Krumpsit and other nuns from Engelthal founded a new monastery at Frauenaurach. This new monastery also flourished and in time prospered in vocations and established yet a new foundation in 1295—the later famous reform monastery of St. Katharine in Nuremberg in 1295.[40] Sadly, by the late Middle Ages the monastery of Engelthal had become simply a home for daughters of the nobility, and the rigor previously practiced and the intensity of private and public prayer diminished. The traditional rules such as those forbidding private possessions, keeping silence as the guardian of prayer, fasting and wearing of the habit gradually ceased to be enforced. Even the enclosure was eventually ignored. The nuns began to go horseback riding for sport and the cloister garden was transformed into a stable for horses. Worst of all, the celebration of Masses for the dead was often forgotten. Several nuns even gave birth to children. Finally, written proof of a love affair between Sr. Barbara Scheiffler and the Dominican prior Johann Heinlein so disgusted the authorities of Nuremberg that reform of the monastery became necessary to restore it to the ideals of Dominican religious life. To begin this reform effort a Dominican visitator arrived on 5 December 1512. He required the restoration of the strict enclosure for the nuns yet modified other monastic rules. However, no movement to reform Engelthal began since the prioress, Margaret of Kürmreuth, opposed it. She went so far as to procure a letter of protection against the reform from Emperor Maximilian I on 23 December 1512. Undaunted, the authorities of the free imperial city of Nuremberg in conjunction with the Master of the Order of Preachers, Thomas de Vio Cajetan, procured a papal bull from Leo X on 9 July 1513 to reform the nuns of Engelthal. The climax of the conflict occurred at seven in the morning on 1 October 1513 when the prior provincial of Germany, the prior of Nuremberg, various city councillors of Nuremberg and numerous other interested parties stormed the monastery of Engelthal having been refused admittance by the nuns. A melée ensued between the nuns of Engelthal and the reformers. Ultimately, the prioress, Margaret Kürmreuth, was sent to St. Katharine, the reform monastery in Nuremberg. The sub-prioress, Martha Kürmreuth, and three other nuns were put in chains. Every sister who held an office was replaced by one of the reforming nuns from St. Katharine. Barbara Tucher became the new prioress. Immediately she requested authority to dispense the remaining unreformed nuns from some of the stricter observances of the Rule. In doing so she, no doubt, hoped to begin the process of gradual reform leading to the unity of reforming and unreformed nuns in the monastery. The reforming nuns of St. Katharine had succeeded using similar methods in renewing other Dominican houses of nuns. They had effectively reformed the monasteries of Maria Medingen in Swabia, Adelhausen near Freiburg, Töss and Ötenbach in Switzerland, Unterlinden in Colmar, and Katharinenthal near

Konstanz.[41] Because of this reform and the renewal of religious spirit the nuns of Engelthal and other monasteries strongly resisted the onslaught of the Protestant Reformation. The nuns of Engelthal and St. Katharine found themselves isolated in overwhelmingly Protestant Nuremberg which had been the first free imperial city to accept the Reformation in 1524 by dictate of the city council. From that time on the the city fathers forbade the nuns in both monasteries from admitting novices. Some nuns, such as the daughter of Veit Stoss, the famous woodcarver of Nuremberg, left the monastery willingly and married a former Dominican priest. In their isolation, the nuns of Engelthal were forced to accept a Lutheran chaplain. By 1530 there were still twenty-four choirsisters in the monastery. While three of them wanted to leave, the other nuns resisted the Protestantization by the city fathers. Christina of Königsfeld, the prioress, wanted to remain loyal to the Catholic Church. In 1565 the last prioress, Anna Tucher, and the last nun, Ursula Zeißen, had to surrender the monastery and its extensive possessions to the civil authorities.[42] Engelthal was closed and with the revenues from the monastery the authorities had the money to establish an academy, later university at Altdorf.[43] With its closing this remarkable place of witness to the power of God's grace to transform human beings into holy beings came to an end.

The nuns' chapel of St. John the Baptist became the Lutheran parish church of the village of Engelthal. Like many medieval German churches it was later modified for the use of the Protestant service and then baroquified. The nuns' choir, where so many extraordinary mystical events had taken place, was made into a balcony. Almost the entire structure of the monastery as rebuilt from 1557-1563 is still extant; only one side of the main cloister is missing. The buildings are currently used as residences, garages and storage facilities for farm equipment. Such is the present condition of what had once been a sublime expression of Dominican monasticism and mysticism.

CHAPTER TWO

Dominican Monasticism

Saint Dominic de Guzman (c. 1171-1221) founded the first monastery of Dominican nuns at Prouille in southern France in 1207. By his preaching he had converted a group of women from the Albigensian heresy and gathered them as a new religious community.[44] Later in 1221 he reformed various groups of nuns into a single monastery at San Sisto in Rome. The basic rule of life of these nuns, called the Primitive Constitutions, was edited by Dominic himself out of a desire to establish Dominican monasticism in a way that would revive among the nuns the apostolic life reported in the Acts of the Apostles. The opening lines and themes of the Primitive Constitutions were taken from the Rule of St. Augustine and also referred to the biblical ideal of apostolic life. "Just as from the very beginning of the early Church the multitude of believers had but one heart and one soul, and placed all that they had in common. so must you also observe the same practices and the same way of life in the house of the Lord."[45] The Friars Preachers had been given the Rule of St. Augustine as their basic document and they added their own usages and customs to this rule. The communities of nuns adopted this rule as well. The Constitutions interpreted the *vita apostolica* as recorded in the Acts of the Apostles in some detail. After the establishment of many new foundations of Dominican nuns throughout Europe it became necessary to revise and adapt the Constitutions to the new state of affairs, making that document the legal and spiritual basis not of a single religious foundation, but of the many and diverse Dominican monasteries of nuns. The task of revising the Constitutions fell to the fifth successor of St. Dominic, Humbert of Romans (c. 1200-1277).

The Constitutions of 1259

Beginning in 1254, Humbert of Romans, the new Master of the Order inherited the care and responsibility of the entire Dominican family, including all those independent monasteries of nuns that had gained association with the friars. Because of his concern for the nuns and their spiritual welfare Humbert promulgated the revised Constitutions for Dominican nuns in 1259. He enjoined the acceptance of the new Constitutions on all monasteries already associated with the Dominican Order and upon all those new communities that wished to align themselves with the Order of Friars Preachers in the future. Humbert made known his intentions for the nuns in his letter of promulgation: "To the devoted Servants of Christ, to all the Sisters confided to the care of the Order of Preachers, Friar Humbert, unprofitable servant of the same Order, wishes you new growth in all the works of salvation."[46] This shows a desire to set the Dominican monastic life in a teleological context in which a sister would practice the observances or "works of salvation" so that she might grow in holiness. The whole purpose of the usages compiled by Humbert from various Dominican monasteries formed the practical and legal basis of the spirituality of Dominican nuns. Humbert made it clear that the practical mysticism outlined here required a nun to understand herself as being in a new relationship to Christ.

> By an admirable effect of Divine Mercy, the Son of the Eternal King has chosen the daughters of men to be His Spouses. Because He is the pattern of all Beauty, He wishes that His betrothed should be pure and beautiful, that they be holy in

body and mind, that no stain appear in them. Since the same Son of God in His infinite bounty has united you indissolubly to Himself by the bonds of religious profession, you should carefully recall with what interior beauty the Spouses of the spotless Lamb should sparkle. What purity, what fragrance should cling to those who wish to enter into the house of the true Asuerus; how becoming it is for those who wish to please such a Spouse to be adorned with virtue and holiness.[47]

Humbert set forth his purpose in greater detail here, writing phrases that linked the sister with Christ using bridal imagery and spousal vocabulary which emphasized the special nature of the sister's relationship to Christ. Given Humbert's teaching, it should not be surprising that Adelheid Langmann and other Dominican writers employed the same constructs and images to conceive of their personal relationship to Christ in a Dominican monastic setting. Adelheid understood herself as a chosen spouse, called to be united with Christ, her bridegroom in holiness and love. She wrote of the beauty of Christ and frequently imaged him as the Lamb. Adelheid also chose to use the image of adornment with virtues as a metaphor for the nun's privileged status as recipient of Christ's grace and also as an image for her growth in perfection, since any adornment, whether in clothing or crowns, symbolized her growth in virtue and in holiness. Adelheid Langmann also re-enforced Humbert's notion of the sister's special powers stemming from this relationship with Christ by referring to King Ahasuerus. Like a king Christ has power and authority over all who are subject to him. The nun, being a spouse of Christ, has the power of Queen Esther to intercede before the king on behalf of others who need his help. Just as Esther found favor with King Ahasuerus (Est. 5:1-8) and was able to save her people, so nuns such as Adelheid Langmann interceded before their divine spouse for the deliverance of souls from purgatory, for the conversion of sinners on earth and for the strengthening in holiness of the elect who already share on earth in the joys of heaven.

Humbert emphasized the importance of beauty and linked the interior beauty of Christ with the attainment of purity and the adornment of virtues in the nun. Mystical union with Christ transforms the nun by Divine Mercy into a holy woman, a spouse of Christ. Descriptive imagery from the Sacred Scriptures reinforces this dynamic. The use of the word "fragrance" links the nun to the bridal imagery of the Song of Songs (Cant. 1:3; 3:6). The reference to the beauty of the spouses of the spotless Lamb who must sparkle with virtue associates the nun with the Book of Revelation and prophesies her inclusion among the elect. The vocabulary of the "marriage feast of the Lamb" corresponds to Humbert's choice of words: "'. . . for the marriage of the Lamb has come, and his Bride has made herself ready; it was granted her to be clothed with fine linen. bright and pure'—for the fine linen is the righteous deeds of the saints." (Rev. 19:6-8 RSV). Humbert places the vocation of the nun freely bound by profession of vows within an eschatological context.

Humbert continued with a description of the characteristics of a Spouse of Christ. A life of virtue leads to the holiness of heaven,

> Courage! Courage! It is this that the Spouse of Christ, modest in her speech, chaste in her affections, immaculate in her thoughts, pure in her intentions, desiring only to please her Spouse, deserves to come to Him, and to hear the words of the divine alliances; to be admitted to the eternal nuptuals, from which the foolish virgins are excluded; and to enjoy forever the vision of Him Whom the Angels desire to contemplate ceaselessly, Whom the multitude of the elect adore and Whom every creature blesses forever and ever.[48]

Humbert's letter contextualized the more mundane and detailed rules in the Constitutions within a spiritual frame and gave the "letter of the Law" life with an eschatological goal in mind. Humbert believed the legal observance of the rules laid down in the Constitutions of such vital importance for fostering personal holiness and for attaining the end of the religious life that he clearly defined association with the Order of Friars Preachers by acceptance of the new Constitutions. He thought that "uniformity observed outwardly in our manners fosters and brings to mind that unity which ought to be preserved inwardly in our hearts."[49]

Having established the theological and eschatological framework of the Constitutions in his Letter, Humbert then delineated the rules by which the Dominican nun should live out her monastic profession. These rules formed the practical mysticism upon which all progress in religious life would be based. The following of these rules concerned all the mystic nuns of the fourteenth century. In the chronicles of the various monasteries, nuns were often portrayed as heroines of observance of the rule. Christina Ebner lauded Christina of Kornburg for her diligence in performing all things necessary in choir.[50] Adelheid of Ingolstadt followed the rule strictly especially with regard to keeping silence.[51] In her *Revelations* Adelheid Langmann praised Sister Elsbet who was rewarded in heaven for going to choir regularly even though she disliked doing it (79).[52] The nuns listened to excerpts from the Constitutions each week while eating in the refectory and were constantly reminded of the connection between the observances and the call to spiritual progress. They were instructed how a nun should conduct herself in the most minute detail. In the Constitutions Humbert established the authority of the prioress in her monastery and detailed every aspect of daily life paying particular attention to prayer (Chapters I-III), fasting (Chapters IV-VII) and silence (Chapter XIII). He devoted five chapters (VIII-XII) to attire, washing etc., three chapters (XIV-XVI) to entrance into the monastery, six chapters (XVII-XXII) to faults and penances for them, and the remaining nine chapters (XXIII-XXXI) to offices, tasks, buildings etc. The nuns adhered to the principles, practice and spirit of the Constitutions which prepared them to be ready for the coming of the Bridegroom.

While the nuns of the Order of Preachers were not deputed to preach as the friars did, both the friars and the nuns shared a common spirituality in the observances of a Dominican monastic life. For the nuns in particular their way of life was very similar to that of the Cistercian nuns. Although mystical experiences may occur wherever the Spirit blows, the nuns and friars of the Dominican Order in the fourteenth century promoted mystical experience by the everyday practice of a monastic life that was meant to bring about ever deeper conversion to Christ and his way of life. The nun should expect to be transformed and made holy by faithfully living according to her monastic vocation.[53] The life of a nun was regulated with the goal of union with Christ in mind. St. Paul encouraged all Christians to use the same kind of effort and sacrifice that an athlete uses to gain a crown of laurel. How much more should the nun strive to "win the race" for an imperishable crown in heaven (1 Cor. 9:24-25)? The daily round of prayers, *lectio divina* and work in a monastery was a grand training program for winning the heavenly crown. Monastic life was conceived as both an ascetic struggle to "put on Christ" (Gal. 3:27) and also as a foretaste of heaven. Monastic life gave witness to the coming of the kingdom of Christ in eternity, where no one will be given in marriage. Their life participated in the praise and glory of God especially through the celebration of the Sacred Mysteries which united the celebration of the Mass on earth with the divine liturgy in heaven

The Monastic Buildings

Monasteries constructed both by friars and by nuns were arranged architecturally to support the goal of monastic life. The most prominent structure in any monastic complex, and also at Engelthal, was the chapel. It occupied fully one side of the main part of the cloister and in height rose above all other parts of the compound. Architecturally it symbolized the reason for the existence of the entire structure and for the kind of life to which the nuns dedicated themselves. The predominance of the chapel preached architecturally that the things of God were preeminently important and that all the rest of life by comparison served only to support contact with God.

For the life of the nuns the most important part of the chapel was the choir, which, at Engelthal, took up two thirds of the area of the chapel. At the center of the monastic combat with temptation and conversion to Christ was the work of God in the choir where the nuns gathered for the celebration of Mass and for the canonical hours of prayer. Every day the nuns chanted the appointed hymns, psalms and canticles at matins, lauds, prime, terce, sext, none, vespers and compline. The Mass at the altar in choir or in chapel was celebrated as the highpoint of their liturgical and spiritual life. Above all the nun believed she met Christ there since he made himself present as God and Man in the Eucharist.[54] In the choir the community of nuns gathered to unite themselves with the universal church, both on earth and in heaven or in purgatory. According to the preface of the Mass, the nuns joined the angels in the praise of the Triune God. In the choir the community heard the Word of God proclaimed and preached. There the individual nun kept vigil in private prayer before the tabernacle containing the Blessed Sacrament. Alone in the choir many nuns had mystical experiences in prayer. Adelheid Langmann mentioned the choir numerous times and often experienced mystical ecstasy there, having to be led away to her cell (21, 22, 36, 72). The choir was that much more important when one considers that the rest of the chapel was not for the use of the nuns, but for the priests and lay people who came to the monastery. The religious life of the nun was centered not in the chapel as such, but in this enclosed portion of the chapel, the choir, cut off from the view of outsiders. The enclosed and usually raised choir also contained articles of devotion— holy pictures of Christ, the Virgin, and other saints. Central to the architectural symbolism was the crucifix as a representation of the all-importance of the sacrifice of Christ on the Cross. The nuns contemplated and celebrated the crucifixion as the turning point in the whole drama of salvation history, since at the moment of Christ's death he showed the totality of his obedience to his Father's will to save the world and the depth of his own love in offering up his life as the new sacrificial Lamb slain for the forgiveness of sins on the altar of the cross. The physical enclosure of the nuns at Engelthal in a cloister garden bounded by the chapel on the north, the dormitory on the east, the refectory on the south and the infirmary on the west symbolized the life cut off from the outside world so that the concentration of the nun's day and every detail of life might serve the goal of growth in Christian life towards union with God. Even the work area was enclosed in a second cloister and the entire monastery itself was surrounded by a wall with three gates by which contact could be made with the outside world. Family members, workers, visitors and dignitaries could gain access to the monastic compound, but not to the cloister, i.e. the enclosure itself. By Rule and by practice the sanctity and privacy of the enclosure was carefully maintained. The Constitutions clearly stated: "Above all else care should be taken that the enclosure should be high and strong, so that there will be no opportunity to pass over it either for coming in or going out of the enclosure. There is to be but one door in the Sister's enclosure, and this door must be strong and solidly locked with at least two or more keys . . . ."[55] The interior open space of the monastery, the cloister, contained a garden and a walkway totally cut off from the view of the world. Walking around this cloister path while meditating symbolized the path of life. The cloister garden itself could symbolize the re-establishment of the garden of Eden, itself a symbol of the perfection of Christian life. It could also represent the enclosed garden where Bride and Bridegroom meet in secret. This garden at the core of the monastery no doubt served as the real basis for much of the visionary imagery employed by the nuns in their chronicles and autobiographies.[56] Adelheid Langmann reported several visions in which a symbolic tree played a significant role (65). She often mentioned flowers with symbolic qualities (62, 88) and the word "garden" was automatically associated with love. Christ told her: "I will lead my Love into the garden of love and will show her the fruit of love and will make her a wreath of white lilies from my divine and human purity and will crown my love and set upon her head a crown of diverse fruits" (62).

The chapter room was the administrative and communication center of the monastery and ranked second in importance only to the chapel. The nuns met in the prayerful environment of the chapter to discuss community matters and work, to be addressed by the prioress on practical and spiritual issues, and when necessary to elect a new prioress. In this room the nuns also proclaimed their own faults against the Rule and accepted penances to perform as a consequence. The Constitutions (chapter XXX) set down the activities proper to the chapter. "Chapter will be held after Matins, or Prime, or Terce and Mass... The community having entered, the reader will read the day of the moon and the Martyrology. The Hebdomadarian will then say the Pretiosa and the rest."[57] After more prayers, "the one who presides will say briefly whatever she thinks appropriate for the good of the house and the correction of the Sisters."[58] Then followed the proclamation of faults, penances and prayers. The chapter room symbolized the democratic ideal of the Dominican Order whose members had always elected their superiors. This room also gave each nun the chance to remember and evaluate her own responsibility toward God and her sisters in a democratic and spiritual community.

The refectory functioned not only as a place of nourishment for the body, but also for the soul. Because of this, meals were taken in silence, accompanied by readings. The arrangement of the refectory as well as the activities performed there reinforced the double nature of nourishment of body and soul. In the refectory the sisters sat at table in precisely the same way that they took their places in the choir. In both rooms the sisters sat according to the order of religion, i.e. by the date of their entry into the monastery, sitting side by side down both sides of the room facing inward. The act of hearing the reading in refectory while eating paralleled the hearing of the Word of God and the eating of the Eucharist during

Mass in the choir. The refectory, like the choir in the chapel, was a holy setting which, while serving to meet the bodily needs of the nun for nourishment, sought more importantly to feed the nun on the spiritual food from the readings. The Constitutions prescribed the proper ritual for meals. "After the Sisters wash their hands, she who presides rings the refectory bell, and then the Sisters will enter. After they have entered, the Versicularian says the *Benedicite* and the community will continue with the prayers for the blessing of the table. The servers, however, begin from the lower end and go up to the Prioress's table."[59] In imitation of the Eucharistic liturgy the meal began with the recitation of public prayers and blessings, and continued with reading during which the meal was served to each sister in her place. Nourishment was generally quite limited for the nuns, and frequently the food was of a poor quality as related in the monastic chronicles and other writings of the nuns. Nuns never ate meat unless with permission for reasons of health. They fasted not only according to the calendar of the church, but kept the great monastic fast from the Exaltation of the Holy Cross (14 September) until Easter. The main meal was served at midday while breakfast and evening collation were little more than snacks.

For spiritual nourishment they listened to all manner of texts among which would be saints' lives such as the *Legenda aurea* by Jacobus de Voragine, the *Vitae Fratrum* by Gerard de Frachet, the *Life of St. Dominic* by Jordan of Saxony or more popularly by Dietrich of Apolda. They might also hear readings from the *Dialogus Miraculum* by Caesarius of Heiterbach, portions of the writings of the Fathers of the Church, various books from the Bible, homilies and regularly the Rule of St. Augustine and the Constitutions of the Order.[60]

Absolute silence reigned in the dormitory where, in the first flowering of Dominican monastic life, all the sisters slept in one room. It seems that the community of Engelthal initially followed this practice, but like most monasteries, eventually provided a cell for the individual nun, especially for the sick. The Constitutions (chapter X) clearly stated that, "No one may be allowed to have a special place to sleep in the community, unless... necessity should require it. In this case at least three Sisters will sleep near one another."[61] In the *Revelations* Adelheid Langmann mentioned both the dormitory and her cell. Upon arising at the call from the exetatrix the nuns recited *The Little Office of the Blessed Virgin Mary* in the Church. This Little Office remained the same, basically, throughout the year and was eventually memorized by the nuns.

Dominicans believed the rule and practice of silence in the monastery to be absolutely necessary for the spiritual welfare of the individual and of the community as a whole. Without exterior and interior silence no spiritual progress could be made and it should not be surprising that the Constitutions emphasized the necessity of silence. "The Sisters will keep silence in the oratory, in the cloister, in the dormitory, and in the refectory. In all other places they may speak with special permission, when and as often as it is permitted."[62] The Constitutions also provided for penances to be performed by those who broke the silence willfully. "If anyone deliberately breaks silence, or gives permission to speak, she will drink water during one dinner and will receive a discipline in the presence of all in Chapter. And from this there is no dispensation, except in the case of the sick who are bedridden."[63] Remarkably in all other cases the Dominican Constitutions always provided for dispensation from rules and did not bind any rule under sin. That the punishment for breaking silence allowed for no dispensation emphasized the importance given to keeping silence. Saint Dominic himself exemplified the practice of keeping silence. The testimony of Brother William of Montferrato for the canonization process of Dominic in 1233 gave to the Order one of the key statements about the character of the founder. "He always observed silence in the times laid down in the Order, and he avoided idle words and spoke always with God or about God."[64] Adelheid Langmann wished to keep all the observances of the Order and frequently spoke of the foolishness of idle conversation preferring, like Saint Dominic, to maintain silence or to pray. Every reform movement of the Dominican Order emphasized the keeping of silence for they believed it to be the primary means to foster an atmosphere of prayer and recollection.

Every part of the monastic complex served the goal of spiritual perfection of the nuns. According to the Constitutions (chapter XXVIII) the "buildings of the Sisters will be humble, not remarkable for their elegance of style or superfluity." However, "great care must be taken to have them so arranged throughout so as to further religious observance as much as possible."[65] The Constitutions also provided for another type of religious observance by providing for a *locatorium*. "Moreover, there should also be, in some proper place, a parlor (*locatorium*) for communicating with outsiders. Here there will be a window with iron gratings similar to that of the larger grille placed in the church."[66] At this window where she was permitted to speak, Adelheid Langmann counseled Marquard Tockler, Eckhart of Hohenstein and Eberhard Schutz.

The Monastic Horarium

Just as the monastic buildings were arranged to foster religious observance so too the horarium functioned to sanctify every moment of the day in a balanced rhythm of community prayer, private prayer, *lectio divina,* labor, eating and sleeping. Of greatest importance for the monastic revival of the *vita apostolica* was the solemn chanting of the psalms, an activity which had always characterized Christian monastic life. The psalm verse, "Seven times a day I praise thee for thy righteous ordinances" (Ps. 119:165 RSV) gave scriptural foundation to the daily sequence of liturgical prayer ceremonies. As mentioned by Adelheid Langmann the nuns gathered in choir for the offices of matins (75, 80, 92), prime (53), terce (53), sext (53), none (53), vespers (15, 21, 22, 44) and compline (51). The Constitutions devoted an entire chapter to the office of the Church (chapter I). "The Sisters assist all together at Matins and at all the canonical hours, unless some are dispensed for a reasonable cause. All the canonical hours must be recited in the church, distinctly and without precipitation, so that the Sisters will not lose devotion and that other duties may not be impeded."[67]

These hours, observed seasonally according to sunrise and sunset, formed the framework of the nun's day around which all other activities took place. Of these activities the most important was the celebration of the Mass, usually after prime. Also the nuns devoted time to private prayer in the choir and to *lectio divina* or the prayerful memorization of scripture and liturgical texts. Each sister had to work in the monastery so that the affairs of the community would run smoothly. A nun may have had to farm, launder, clean, copy manuscripts, take care of all the liturgical accoutrements, and perform any task necessary to support the life and mission of the community. One of the hardest practices was the singing of the office of Matins because it interrupted the time for sleep in the middle of the night.

Even as the day was divided by the canonical hours of prayer, so the year progressed according to liturgical seasons and feast days. In the autobiographies and biographies of the fourteenth century this annual cycle of feasts and fasts gave a definite liturgical rhythm to life for the nuns. The two great seasons of the liturgical year were Advent/Christmas and Lent/Easter. The Advent season brought special grace to Margaret Ebner. Good Friday was the climax of the Lenten fast and the Passion cycle. Adelheid Langmann and Christina Ebner frequently made references to feast days and ecclesiastical seasons. The nuns always lived in anticipation of the coming feast especially Christmas and Easter.

Monastic practices

Dominicans professed obedience as the primary vow. They considered the vows of poverty and chastity as part of obedience. And so according to the Dominican profession formula the nun promised only obedience.

> I, _____, make profession and promise obedience to God, to the Blessed Mary, and to the Blessed Dominic, and to you, _____, Prioress, in the place of _____, Master of the Order of Friars Preachers, according to the rule of Blessed Augustine and the Constitutions of the Sisters whose care is committed to the Order of Preachers that I will be obedient to you and to my other Prioresses until death.[68]

Obedience was utterly important because it most perfectly imitated the virtue of Christ himself who, by dying on the cross, offered total conformity of his will to that of the Father by "obediently accepting even death—death on a cross" (Phil. 2:8). The consent of his human will and the shedding of his blood constituted the sacrifice by which Christ saved the world. By comparison, poverty and chastity seemed relatively less important for the imitation of Christ. However, poverty as a guiding ideal of Saint Dominic and the Order helped to separate the nun from the things and people of the world and from attachment to them. Adelheid Langmann and the people whom she advised constantly needed to choose between God's will and the world. Poverty then served as an aid in achieving the necessary detachment from the world in order to cling to the things of God. Chastity was more than something practical—it functioned as an eschatological symbol of the nun's attachment to God and to the things of God, and showed a preference for the things of heaven over earthly things.

Although a library catalogue exists for the monastery of Engelthal, no list of refectory readings survives.[69] It is clear what books the nuns possessed, but unknown which ones were read in refectory during meals. However, sample lists of readings do exist from Engelthal's daughter house, St. Katharine in Nuremberg. Since close ties existed between the two houses, the list of readings at St. Katharine offers a glimpse into what may have been done at almost any Dominican monastery.[70] This list only hints at what may have been read at Engelthal since it was drawn up for another monastery for the years 1429-31. The recommendations for reading were carefully worked out using numerous books from the extensive library at St. Katharine's. In general, for a particular feast day the appointed epistle and gospel would be read along with a sermon on the day and perhaps a devotional work appropriate to the theme. For example, on Pentecost Sunday at the first meal the epistle "In those days . . ." was read followed by the *Veni Creator*; then the Gospel of the day, followed by a reading from the Book of Prophets "There is a question . . . ." Then a reading taken from the Song of Songs, "Rise up rushing wind . . ." and a reading beginning with *Spiritus sanctus hodie* followed by sermons by John Tauler: *Qui spiritans puer iste erit, Emitte spiritum tuum, Qui spiritu Dei*; and finally a reading from the Acts of the Apostles, presumably the text reporting the Pentecost event.[71]

The plan for readings covered the entire liturgical year and included readings from all the Gospels plus the Gospel of Nicodemus, the Acts of the Apostles, Paul's First Letter to the Corinthians, the Song of Songs, unspecified prophetic books and the Apocalypse; liturgical texts such as the *Exultet*; sermons by John Tauler, St. Gregory, St. Thomas; and other sorts of texts: the Rule of St. Augustine, the Constitutions of the Sisters, and devotional works such as "On the Name of Jesus" and a life of St. Dominic. These readings were taken from manuscripts at hand in the monastery library. It should also be noted that the texts chosen were not only in Latin. Frequently the Gospel, Epistle, homily or tract were in German, making it more likely that the hearers would learn from the readings. Adelheid Langmann made no reference to reading, *lectio divina*, or study in her *Revelations*, yet her use of scripture quotes and allusions as well as the numerous resonances of the sermons of Bernard of Clairvaux, the writings of Mechthild of Magdeburg, *The Song of the Daughter of Zion*, and other religious works, make it clear that she learned much from these influential texts and made use of them in her life and literary work. Of particular note with regard to the education of Adelheid Langmann is the fact that excerpts from the Song of Songs occurred more frequently in the cycle of refectory readings than did other Scriptural texts. It is likely that this was also the practice at Engelthal and may account for Adelheid's numerous references to the biblical text.

Dominican monastic life as regulated by the Rule of St. Augustine and especially by the Constitutions of the Sisters formed the practical mysticism of nuns such as Adelheid Langmann, which disposed her and others to experience the ecstatic mysticism described in her *Revelations*. These texts and the spirit of religious fervor of the age established an ideal of mystical life unparalleled in the history of Christianity.

Mystical Life as Ideal

The religious fervor of the fourteenth century brought about a culture and an atmosphere in which mystical life of an ecstatic sort became idealized. Martin Grabmann portrayed the mystics of that time in a favorable light. "These were the mystics . . . who yearned for knowledge of God and the love of God and who strove by leading a life of virtues to be as united with God as was possible on earth. They set down their religious inner life in compelling writings."[72] This ideal of ecstatic mystical life occurred among Dominicans along the Rhine, the Danube and in the region of Franconia, especially at the monasteries of Töss and Ötenbach in Switzerland, Katharinenthal near Konstanz, Unterlinden in Colmar, Adelhausen near Freiburg in Breisgau, Maria Medingen in Swabia and Engelthal near Nuremberg. In fact, almost all written evidence of *Frauenmystik* in the fourteenth century comes from the Dominican Order.[73] In all of these Dominican monasteries of nuns discipline of life was the ideal in order to nurture spiritual growth even to a mystical level. This discipline also grounded mystical experience in the liturgical routine of the daily round of prayers and praise offered by the whole community.

Hieronymus Wilms theorized about the rise of mysticism and gave several reasons why such a unique flowering of mysticism should occur in the German-speaking lands in the fourteenth century and why Dominican women and men should play such a major role. Wilms believed that the age fostered a turning away from earthly cares to heavenly matters since that entire period of church history was so tragic for several reasons. At that time the popes ruled from Avignon rather than Rome, and were therefore under the influence of the French kings. The conflict between emperor and pope and especially the interdict imposed upon the lands subject to Emperor Louis the Bavarian, with the subsequent imperial reaction supported by the theories of Franciscan Spirituals, tested the loyalties of every Christian and brought many faithful people into confusion or indifference. Also natural causes contributed to the malaise of the times—famine, earthquakes, floods, strange diseases, comets and prophecies about them, and the Black Death.[74] While all these reasons bear social and political importance they really do not fully explain the incredible spiritual movement of that time. In fact, most of the reports about mystical life and experiences of Dominican nuns were written prior to the ravages of the Black Death. The Bubonic plague took the lives of many nuns and monks and actually destroyed the fabric of religious life in the monasteries and consequently aided in diminishing or even destroying the monastic culture that fostered mysticism. The reasons for this flowering of German mysticism had more to do with the preaching of Dominicans and the educational level of the nuns than with social, political, or natural influences.

Other scholars proffer different reasons why mystical life developed so powerfully in Dominican cloisters. Some ascribed this development to the influence of Meister Eckhart, Henry Suso and Mechthild of Magdeburg, while others attributed it to the practical mysticism of the nuns expressed in their use of the Divine Office, *The Little Office of the Blessed Virgin Mary*, the reading of the Church Fathers, *The Song of the Daughter of Zion*, the practice of *lectio divina* and contact with the friars.⁷⁵ I believe that all of these factors contributed to setting the stage for a flowering of mystical life, but they do not explain why mystical life flourished in Dominican monasteries of the fourteenth century. The nuns and friars of the time would more than likely have ascribed the entire mystical movement to God's providence. The task of the nun was to dispose herself to the action of divine grace for the process of divinization. They considered themselves to be recipients of God's special graces and as his special friends chosen to enjoy intimacy with God. This belief arose from the mutual influence of the friars and the nuns and had much to do with the advancement of learning.

Many nuns in these monasteries enjoyed a high level of education and could read Latin.⁷⁶ They used Latin in all the religious ceremonies and therefore were familiar with that language and showed in their writings that they understood it. Also, they possessed and studied copies of theological works such as the *Summa Theologica* by St. Thomas Aquinas and *The Flowing Light of the Godhead* by Mechthild of Magdeburg, among others. The secular priest, Henry of Nördlingen, translated Mechthild's work, sent copies to Margaret Ebner at Maria Medingen and possibly to Christina Ebner at Engelthal.⁷⁷ Christina Ebner mentioned *The Flowing Light of the Godhead* twice in her *Revelations,* showing that she was familiar with that text. In the summer of 1346 she related that God spoke to her: "My eternal Love, I have sent you the book that is called an outflowing light of the Godhead before your death so that you will become even bolder."⁷⁸ During Easter week in 1348 she related the following words from God: "I have sent you that book so that your spiritual joy and hope be the more increased. And I meant the book that is called an outflowing light of the Godhead."⁷⁹ Other scholars have also claimed that Adelheid Langmann was influenced by Mechthild's book. Wilhelm Preger stated that the book was sent to Engelthal in 1345 and that certain details suggest Mechthild's influence: Adelheid's singular desire for God described in contrast to the inadequacy of consolation from heaven, earth and angels and the insistent request that God come to console her without any intermediaries (41, 42).[80] Also Siegfried Ringler believed that certain portions of the *Revelations* of Adelheid Langmann were written under the influence of Mechthild of Magdeburg.[81]

That the Dominican nuns who took part in this flowering of mysticism were educated in spiritual matters there can be no doubt. Sufficient evidence has been given to note some of the texts they possessed and used in their own writings. In her *Revelations* Adelheid Langmann showed knowledge especially of the Song of Songs (1,4), the Gospel of John (2,4,8,12,18), The Gospel of Luke (1,2,4,7,22), the Gospel of Matthew (3,26) and the Book of Revelation (3). She also knew St. Bernard's sermons *On the Song of Songs* since she employed allusions to and direct quotes from them in her book (42, etc.).

The level of education of the Dominican nuns also had to do with the influence of the Dominican friars. The *cura monialium* was given only to highly educated and gifted Dominican priests. "The best of the Dominican preachers... found in the monasteries of Dominican nuns a grateful audience for their religious zeal."[82] These preachers, among whom were John Tauler and Henry Suso, spoke of the love of God in less speculative terms, appealing to the emotions and affections of the audience. These preachers were also aware, especially because of the training given Dominican preachers and the advice from Humbert of Romans, that they should direct their preaching and formulate its content and expression according to the abilities and spiritual maturity of the audience.[83] Hence a sermon delivered to the general public in the city square on a Sunday afternoon differed greatly from what could be preached to a community of nuns. The audience is different and so the context as well as the content and the mode of expression of the preaching must be different. Even with the nuns, the emphasis would be on a practical mysticism which should be experienced by the hearer. There was nothing pedantically academic about the mysticism preached. The message of the sermon was not meant to be discussed and politely critiqued over a glass of Rhine wine; rather it was meant to be applied directly to the conditions of the life of the sisters. Because of the level of education and religious observance of the nuns, the preacher's words, like the seed in the parable of the sower, found fertile ground in the minds and hearts of the Dominican nuns.

The preaching of the friars focused on several indispensable themes which then fashioned and supported the ideal of life of a Dominican nun. The nuns were to renounce all earthly things in both a material and a spiritual sense. In order to make spiritual progress the nuns had to renounce the false Self completely so that they could live in the truth. As all Christians needed to do, the nuns had to pick up their cross in imitation of Christ and proceed along the "narrow way" by growing in the practice of virtues. This was the way to mystical experience of seeing God "face to face."[84] Even in the present life in the monastery moments of union with Christ could occur during which all cares, worries and self-consciousness would disappear. The human spirit, in rapture ("out of itself"), sees God and forgets self. This rapture which both Saint Paul and Moses experienced represents the highest happiness in this life. For this the mystic longed—the experience of God in knowledge and love.[85] Like the athlete who sacrificed all to gain merely a laurel wreath, the mystic sacrificed all earthly things to gain all heavenly things.

The Influence of the Friars: Eckhart, Tauler and Suso

The nuns received guidance in their mystical progress from the friars who preached to them, the most famous of whom were Meister Eckhart, John Tauler and Henry Suso. All three visited various monasteries of nuns where they preached, taught and counseled them. Of these three friars, Meister Eckhart had the least direct influence on the nuns. Yet, for instance, when one compares Otto Langer's analysis of Eckhart's influence,

Adelheid Langmann's writing and experience do coincide with the influence of Eckhart. According to Otto Langer, Eckhart's teachings diverged significantly from the teachings gleaned from the various Sister-Books in four significant areas: 1) The religious conversion (*ker*) of the nun signified a new beginning or new existence for the nun. In the Sister-Books this change is an interior act symbolized by the flight from the world and the entrance into a monastery. For Eckhart, however, "the real new beginning of life consists not in a flight into the monastery, but rather in the breaking of self-will."[86] The nun's problem was not with the world, but with herself. While Adelheid Langmann wrote extensively about her entrance into the monastery, she never portrayed it as a flight from the world. In fact, she resisted Christ's will for her to enter Engelthal and could only be induced to take the veil because of revelations received by herself and by a friend. Her entry into the monastery was an act of obedience to the will of Christ. The entire pattern of Adelheid's spiritual growth approximated more closely Otto Langer's description of Meister Eckhart's teachings. Adelheid struggled with her self-will and, even though desirous of conforming her will to Christ's, she continually grappled with this problem. Even though Adelheid prayed to conform her will to Christ's will (142), she could not do it. After a series of revelations in which Christ asked her to choose between going to heaven or remaining on earth, she finally responded, "I want whatever you want (32)." This, finally, was the right answer. Christ immediately delivered his lengthiest response thus far in the *Revelations* and rewarded Adelheid with association with his mother, saints and angels, because she had finally conformed her will to his. Likewise, Margarethe Weinhandl emphasized the importance of conformity of will for the nuns as demonstrated in the Sister-Books.[87]

2) The ascetic practices or penitential observances (*uebunge*) as presented in the Sister-Books showed a tendency to destroy the body, the greater extent of which would lead to greater happiness.

Eckhart distinguished the external work of penance from the intention. Love, rather than severe penances, is the measure of perfection. "The real penitential work is the destruction of the (false) Self, the only good is a good will."[88] Adelheid Langmann, while she practiced the normal penances prescribed by the Constitutions of the Sisters and also practiced severe penance in the form of the discipline, clearly did such things precisely as a "discipline" to destroy her false self, and her motive was always love for Christ, not the desire for self-inflicted torture. Through her revelations Adelheid learned to connect suffering and love as the perfect imitation of Christ who suffered and died on the cross motivated by love for his Father whose salvific will he was fulfilling, and love for all those who would be saved by his sacrificial death. Christ taught her, "Gladly bear suffering for my sake. See what I have suffered for you (25)." In another revelation the virgin *Caritas* teaches her about Christ's love. "Love compelled him to give himself into the hands of his enemies and let himself be martyred in such anguish and need that no one can ponder it" (72). *Caritas* went on to explain every moment of the passion as done out of love. "When he died out of love, his side was pierced and water and blood flowed from it. This he gives as a gift to all those who love him" (72).

3) Using a term from von Balthasar, Langer claimed that Eckhart would prefer an "*Entphantasierung des Glaubens*" or "a faith stripped of images" as opposed, apparently, to the visions and private revelations granted to the nuns. Adelheid Langmann reported almost innumerable visions and revelations throughout the text in dialogue form. For her the imaginative power of fantasy supported what was even more important to Eckhart's mysticism—a union of God and the soul at the level of being. Adelheid imaged this union primarily in the heart. On her heart Christ wrote his name never to be erased (15, 25, 32, 117). Mary placed her child in Adelheid's heart. "Our Lady placed herself in front of the sister and it seemed to this sister [Adelheid] that her own heart opened up and Our Lady took her little Child and

placed him in her heart. When her heart closed up again Our Lady made the sign of the cross over her heart saying, 'You will remain in this heart forever' (50)." Further, Adelheid prayed to Christ, "Dearly beloved Lord, for the sake of the love that you showed me yesterday, let me see you" (25). Christ responded simply, "Look into your own heart" (25). These non-bridal images reinforce the idea that Adelheid and Christ are united at the very core of her being, a much more Eckhartian approach than evidence gleaned from the Sister-Books would allow.

4) Langer's fourth differentiation between the mystical teachings in the Sister-Books and those of Meister Eckhart had to do with the role of ecstasy. Ecstasy played no role in Eckhart's mysticism. The human person should live as a "Son of God" according to his human nature which has attained an inestimable dignity by the incarnation of God.[89] If Langer was correct in his description of Eckhart's teaching, clearly Adelheid Langmann's ecstatic mysticism has no connection with his thought. Her ecstasies were important as signs of spiritual progress and formed her relationship to Christ as bride and bridegroom, lover and beloved.

John Tauler, a disciple of Meister Eckhart, had a more personal and lasting impact on the nuns. He exercised his ministry of the care of souls in his native Strasbourg and had frequent contact with the seven monasteries of Dominican nuns in the city. In addition he exerted a wide influence on monasteries elsewhere, and on the Friends of God. His only extant letter was written to Margaret Ebner, a nun and mystic at Maria Medingen in Swabia.[90] Christina Ebner, a nun of Engelthal spoke of Tauler's "fiery tongue that kindled the entire world."[91] Of the three great German friar mystics considered here "Tauler is the one who has exercised the greatest influence on the German-speaking countries as well as on the rest of Europe."[92] A Carthusian, Laurentius Surius, translated Tauler's works into Latin in 1548. In his dedicatory preface he wrote of Tauler:

> Tauler's attraction lies in the fact that he (who certainly had reached the heights of Christian perfection) never tires to encourage all, as strongly as possible, in the love of God and neighbor; that he exhorts them to eradicate vice, to be attentive to their innermost ground, to strive for virtue and to deny their self-will and inordinate desires; that he invites them to imitate Christ by taking up His Cross and following Him humbly but faithfully in spite of many obstacles and mortifications; until finally the soul becomes so united to Him as to be one spirit with Him, in a most wondrous way. All this is nothing else but loving God with heart and soul and mind, with all one's strength, and one's neighbor as oneself.[93]

This approach differs greatly from Eckhart's more cerebral *Entphantisiering des Glaubens* for it stressed the path of identification with the passion of Christ, and of union with Christ's perfect humanity so that the believer may come to know Christ in his divinity. Tauler directed his Sermon 59 "*Ego si exaltatus fuero*" for the feast of the Exaltation of the Holy Cross (14 September) to an audience of cloistered religious women, presumably at one of the monasteries in Strasbourg. He preached to the sisters about bearing the cross within themselves in imitation of Jesus:

> We meet people who indeed carry the Cross outwardly, performing good and pious exercises and having taken upon themselves the burden of monastic life. They do a lot of chanting and reading, they take their place in choir and in the refectory, but they do our Lord a minor service because they are only externally involved. Do you suppose that God has created you like so many songbirds? You were to be his beloved brides and spouses.[94]

Tauler preached a lesson on the interiorization of the monastic observances. It was not enough to take up the cross externally (enter the monastery, chant psalms etc.), the cross should also be taken up internally. Speaking to the sisters he admonished them to "accept this cross from God and bear it in the depth of your heart."[95] He furthered his argument using images, examples and quotes from scripture and the Fathers and Doctors of the Church. He showed concern that the sisters learn the ways of the mystical life correctly in order to persevere in the true practice of monastic observances which would lead to an interior change in the individual nun helping her to live more closely united to Christ. In fact, the nun is destined to become a beloved bride and spouse of Christ.

While Tauler preached extensively about Christian life and mysticism to the nuns, Henry Suso apparently lived more in keeping with those teachings and seems to have identified with the nuns in ways not expressed by Eckhart or Tauler. In style and content, Suso's writings were closer to the kind of literature produced by the nuns when writing biographies or autobiographies such as the various *Revelations*. His biography was written by a nun of the monastery of Töss, Elsbeth Stagel, and, like the autobiographies of Margaret Ebner, Adelheid Langmann and Christina Ebner, offers a more complete account of the life than those offered of the nuns in the Sister-Books of the monasteries. Suso's one-hundred meditations and petitions resemble the prayers of Margaret Ebner and Adelheid Langmann, although thematically he concentrated solely on the passion of Christ rather than on events from the course of Christ's entire life as preferred by the nuns.[96] Events from Suso's life matched similar mystical experiences of Adelheid Langmann. He underwent a spiritual espousal with Eternal Wisdom (Chapter 3) whereas Adelheid was espoused to Christ her beloved (32). Suso branded the name of Jesus on his heart (chapter 4) whereas Christ wrote his name on Adelheid's heart (15, 25). Suso's use of images and choice of vocabulary resonated with those used by the nuns. Quotes from Suso's *The Soul's Love-Book*" might just as easily have been written by a nun.

Open my heart for the sake of your precious blood, so that I may behold you, King of kings and Lord of lords, with the eyes of faith. Place all my understanding and wisdom in your wounds, so that henceforth I may draw closer to your death and cut myself off from all earthly things until at last it will be no longer I that live, but you who live in me and by me. Thus, bound with the cords of love, I will remain ever fixed in you.[97]

All three of these Dominican preachers, as representative of many others, ministered to Dominican nuns by preaching and teaching. Each left a legacy of benefit for their sisters: Eckhart's example and inspiration to Tauler and Suso, Tauler's preaching and instruction on religious life, Suso's experiential compatibility with the sensibilities of the nuns. Each helped to bring to life and to direct a monastic culture that supported a flourishing of mysticism in a positive way. The reason for this extraordinary flowering in the fourteenth century has more to do with faith than with social, political or natural circumstances. The preachers and the nuns believed that nothing was impossible with God. With that belief mysticism and mystical experiences as recorded by the nuns abounded.

Mystical Phenomena

Among numerous possible mystical phenomena Margarete Weinhandl ascertained eleven mystical motifs common among Dominican nuns of the fourteenth century: 1) the appearance of God and the saints at the deathbed; 2) the gift of tears; 3) Mary's mantle of protection; 4) the ability to perceive the spiritual state of others; 5) the comparison of the Order with a garden; 6) the promise to appear after death; 7) the appearance of a dead sister and her relation of her state after death; 8) the certitude of eternal life promised by God or revealed through a saint; 9) all kinds of miracles associated with the host or with receiving communion;

10) the illumination or transfiguration of the face or body; and 11) the yearning for particular graces.[98] Adelheid Langmann experienced or longed for many of these phenomena herself. 1) God the Father assured her, "Be at peace. I will free you from the prison of your body and take you up into my divine grace and will lead you into the kingdom that I prepared for you from the beginning of the world (55)." 2) Adelheid often shed "sweet" tears and prayed for this gift, "I remind you (Christ) that you cried and ask you to give me sweet tears of love for all my sins" (116). Christ directed her to take the discipline so that she would "cry sweet tears" (52). 3) Kunigunde, Adelheid's nanny, related mystical events from Adelheid's childhood. "Then the most beautiful lady . . . came and she was wearing a blue mantle. This mantle was so wide that if it had ever been unfolded it would have covered the whole world" (67). 4) Adelheid frequently perceived the spiritual state of others despite a lack of cooperation on the part of her advisees. When Marquard Tockler refused to reveal his problem, Adelheid stated simply, "You are sorely tempted. I know for certain you want to kill yourself" (60). 5) Garden imagery occurred frequently throughout the work. Adelheid referred to fruits and various flowers by name and wrote of the garden of love, but did not directly apply this imagery to the monastery. 6 & 7) Adelheid never promised to appear after her death, but another sister after she had died, Elsbet, did appear to Adelheid to reveal, "God is so merciful and did such good for me at my end that, if I had known this, I would never have had such great anxiety about my death" (79). 8) Adelheid received certitude of eternal life directly from God the Father. "I will . . . lead you into the kingdom that I prepared for you from the beginning of the world" (55). 9) Adelheid also reported various miracles with regard to the host. Christ succeeded in convincing her to enter the monastery because she could not swallow the host until she promised to become a nun (5). Also, while a priest was celebrating Mass the Christ Child appeared and changed into the host (30).

Adelheid had a variety of mystical experiences such as mystical marriage, transport into purgatory and heaven, the writing of the name of Jesus on her heart, mystical lactation, visions, locutions and holy fragrances. She spoke with God the Father, the Son and the Holy Spirit, the Virgin Mary, St. John the Beloved, St. Peter and other saints. She visited or was visited by deceased members of her family and other souls. She fell into ecstasy and had to be led away to her cell. She lay like a corpse overwhelmed with revelations. Above all she heard innumerable times the salutation of love from Christ, "My Beloved!"

Such mystical experiences were considered to be the natural outcome of a nun's spiritual development if she were faithful to the Dominican way of life and allowed herself to be formed in prayer and ascetical practices. That the nun would progress in holiness, symbolized by mystical experiences was expected. Margarethe Weinhandl agreed with Engelbert Krebs concerning the kind of life the nuns led and quoted him: ". . . a nun who entered the monastery in its first flowering, took on a life full of exalted spiritual activity. If she was fervent, she filled her mind and her feelings with heavenly things taken daily from the Holy Scripture, the Fathers, poets, teachers, from the particularly poetic Dominican liturgy and from the innumerable legends of the saints and stories of the history of the Order . . . ."[99] As recorded in her *Revelations* Adelheid clearly lived in such a manner.

CHAPTER THREE

Scriptural Influences

Adelheid Langmann demonstrated certain and familiar knowledge of scriptural passages in her *Prayer* and in her *Revelations*. The entire *Prayer* focused on details from the life of Christ taken from the canonical and non-canonical Gospels, and elsewhere. She quoted from the Gospel of Luke, the epistles of Paul and from the Song of Songs. Her knowledge of scripture came not from academic study, but from monastic immersion in the biblical texts that told of the life of Jesus Christ. The Song of Songs and the Book of Revelation had the greatest impact on Adelheid's thought and visionary imagination.

There is no way to exaggerate the importance of the biblical Songs of Songs for mystics of the fourteenth century. This book or numerous texts based on it had circulated and been copied throughout the monasteries of Europe. The *Hohelied* written in 1063 by Abbot Williram of Ebersberg made a paraphrase of the Song of Songs available to German-speaking readers.[100] The *St. Trutperter Hohelied* composed in the twelfth century continued to make the text of the Song of Songs available. The biblical text was also available in the German language, as evidenced by the extant Wenzelbibel and others. In addition the nuns sang and heard portions of the Song of Songs in antiphons and other liturgical texts, especially from the *Little Office of the Blessed Virgin* which the nuns recited every day, and eventually committed this office to memory, The Dominican nuns also listened to readings from the Song of Songs in refectory. So, for example, the nuns of St. Katharine Monastery, a daughter house of Engelthal, listened to chapters of the Song of Songs read in refectory fourteen times during the year. They heard chapters one and two during Advent equating the yearning of the Bride with the longing of the Hebrew people for the coming of the Messiah. On Christmas Eve chapter 6 was read. The nuns heard "I am my beloved's and my beloved is mine (Cant. 6:3) and may have seen in the incarnation and birth of Jesus the union of the Savior and his people. Chapters three and four were read aloud on Pentecost perhaps leading the nuns to reflect upon the power of the coming of the Spirit and the indescribable effect that experience had on the apostles and could have on the nuns. When the nuns meditated on chapter five on the Solemnity of Corpus Christi they could well have seen in the appearance and hiddenness of the Bridegroom a foreshadowing of the real presence of Christ in the Eucharist, who, nonetheless is still veiled in mystery until the Last Day.[101]

Correlations between the Song of Songs and Adelheid Langmann's *Revelations* occur through paraphrase, terms of address, the motif of love-sickness, and the use of garden imagery. In a revelation from the Lord during Mass on the summer solstice Adelheid heard, "My Beloved, your mouth is sweeter than pure honey. Honey and milk are under your tongue." (35) This is directly reminiscent of Cant. 4:11: "Your lips distil nectar, my bride; honey and milk are under your tongue." On the octave of the Dedication of the Church she was addressed in a similar way, "My Beloved, my Tender One, my Beautiful One, my love-sweet dear One, under your tongue is honey." (41) This revelation followed immediately upon the interview with the high-ranking preacher who confirmed the validity of Adelheid's thought and experience and commanded her to write down all that had happened to her. His encouragement served as a divine affirmation of Adelheid's experience and a confirmation that she must speak of the Lord's mystical marriage to her. That

Adelheid paraphrased texts from the fourth chapter of the *Song of Songs*, demonstrates the importance of that chapter for her imagery and the understanding of her relationship to Christ, the Beloved. Further, the Lord himself preached to her in terms very close to those used in that same chapter: "Your mouth smells of roses and your body of violets. You are altogether beautiful for nothing is lacking in you"(42). The comparison of the Beloved with lovely things is characteristic of the terms of address in the Song of Songs, but more important here is the idea of perfection. "You are all fair, my love, there is no flaw in you" (Cant. 4:7 RSV). The Bridegroom echoed this theme when he addressed the Bride, "My dove, my perfect one . . ." (Cant. 6:9). In her own *Prayer* Adelheid expressed this ideal of perfection as an important part of her theological worldview. Speaking of the Virgin Mary, she prayed, "I remind you, Lord, that the angel found her perfect in holiness and that you had sanctified her so that she was without sin because she was always overflowing with all grace. And so I ask you to bring me to all perfection and fill me up with all graces so that nothing will be lacking in me and you will find me ready at all times when you come" (98). Heavenly personages promised to shower gifts upon Adelheid: the Holy Spirit declared to her, "I will make you so perfect with my divine goodness that nothing will be lacking in you" (55). The Virgin Mary addressed God asking for a gift for Adelheid. "Lord, you who bring about all good things, and have also made me perfect in all things, give me something out of your goodness for this person today" (48). The Holy Spirit also promised, "I will never cease from granting her my goodness until she becomes the most perfect of all human beings" (48). Christ himself chastised her for doubting his perfection asserting, "There is nothing lacking in me" (43). Adelheid responded immediately, "Lord, I see nothing lacking in you" (43). Not only did the idea of perfection in holiness (nothing lacking) identify Adelheid with Mary, but with Christ himself. Adelheid's prayer for perfection, and the Holy Spirit's promise assured her position among the elect, the Christ-like, whose first member was Mary.

Terms of Address

Terms of address used by Adelheid Langmann in her *Revelations* echo those found in the Song of Songs. As the Bridegroom addressed the Bride so does Christ address Adelheid. On the feast of the Epiphany Christ promised to make Adelheid his bride, "I will make you my bride today so that I will never be separated from you. I will show you all the loyalty that a lover gives to the Beloved. I marry you today so that I will always remain with you and I will do everything that you wish" (19). He continued this bridal vocabulary saying, "Every bridegroom gives a wedding band, so I have married you by giving you my body" (20). He addressed her as "Beloved" (27, 35, 36, 38, 43, 51, 72) or "Love" (41, 56, 62, 65, 76). He also used extended terms of address reminiscent of the Song of Songs: "My Love, my Tender One, my Spouse" (32), "My Darling, my Tender One, my Spouse and my Sister and my Child" (35), "My Beloved, my Tender One, my Betrothed, and my dear Spouse and my dear Child" (37), "My Beloved, my Tender One, my Beautiful One, my love-sweet dear One" (41), "My Beloved, sweet as sugar or honey, my Tender One, my Pure One" (63), "My Beloved, my Love and my Tender One" (81). Such terms of endearment frequently occur in the Song of Songs. "Behold, you are beautiful, my love; behold, you are beautiful" (Cant. 1:15, 4:1 RSV), "Arise my love, my fair one" (Cant. 2:10 RSV), "my sister, my bride" (Cant. 4:9, 4:10, 4:12, 5:1 RSV), "my sister, my love, my dove, my perfect one" (5:2 RSV), "My dove, my perfect one" (Cant. 6:9 RSV). Adelheid extended use of these terms of address and amplified them in mystical ecstasy. Her use of such terms clearly shows her identification with the Bride and her special relationship with the Bridegroom who is Christ.

The Motif of Love-sickness

Adelheid Langmann also used the motif of love-sickness found in the Song of Songs. There the Bride professed, "I am sick with love" (Cant. 2:5 RSV). Later, when she could not find her beloved she asked the daughters of Jerusalem, "if you find my beloved, . . . tell him I am sick with love" (Cant. 5:8 RSV). Adelheid mentioned an undisclosed sickness several times. In her *Prayer* while meditating upon the Three Kings she implored the Lord to guide her with love "and not with suffering" since he knew all about her sickness (119). However, Adelheid spoke of her love-sickness while relating the episode of being guided on a lengthy and arduous journey by *Spes* and *Caritas* to meet her Beloved. After Adelheid had weakened considerably by the rigors of the journey, *Spes* and *Caritas* asked her, "Lady, what is wrong with you that you are so sick? What are you yearning for?" To this question Adelheid responded, "I am yearning for him who is Lord of all lords and God of all gods, for my only beloved Love Jesus Christ. If he does not come to me I must die . . . I must die of painful longing for him" (72). Her love-sickness also derives from her fear of abandonment. In the *Revelations* Christ constantly affirmed that he would "never be separated" (5, 14, 19, 46, 50) from Adelheid, and asserted that "Just as little as I can ever be separated from my Father, so little will I ever be separated from you" (24). This astounding comparison between the unity of Father and Son with the union of Christ and Adelheid brings the relationship of Christ and Adelheid to an unheard of level. Yet Adelheid also believed that Christ often played at abandoning her and because of this belief she had to be reassured by Ulrich, the prior of Kaisheim, that this was simply *minnespil*, a game of love. "Often he [Christ] will act as if to play at betraying you and wanting to abandon you or to drive you away. Pay no heed. Believe me, it is his intention for you to act more tenderly and kindly" (159). The *minnespil* only goes to intensify and deepen their ardent yearning and mutual love.

Imagery of a Private Space: the Garden and the Lady's Chamber

The *Revelations* (42) and the Song of Songs (4, 5, 7) share the imagery of a private space—both a lady's chamber (*kemenate*) and an enclosed garden. In the biblical text the Bridegroom compared his Beloved to a garden: "A garden locked is my sister, my bride, a garden locked, a fountain sealed" (Cant. 4:12 RSV); ". . . a garden fountain, a well of living water, and flowing streams from Lebanon" (Cant. 4:15 RSV). He professed, "I will come to my garden, my sister, my bride" (Cant. 5:1 RSV) and knocked at the gate saying, "Open to me, my sister, my love, my dove, my perfect one . . ." (Cant. 5:2 RSV). In a similar space, a vineyard, the Bridegroom promised, "There I will give you my love" (Cant. 7:12 RSV). Adelheid Langmann also used the imagery of an enclosed space when writing about a revelation while listening to preaching. After telling Adelheid that she was all beautiful for there was "nothing lacking" in her, Christ went on to describe their relationship echoing the Song of Songs. Speaking to Adelheid, Christ said, "You have captured me, just like a maiden who holds a young man captive in a lady's chamber and who knows well that if his friends were aware of it they would kill her and him" (42). The entrapment seems mutual, for when asked what had forced Christ to enter the enclosed space, he responded, "Your beauty has drawn me" (42). In turn he asked why he had been permitted to enter. Adelheid responded, "It is the great love that I bear for you." Just as the Bride in the Song of Songs was compared to a garden, so Adelheid was this enclosed space and she alone had the key to allow or to forbid entrance. Christ said to her, "See, thus have you captured me in the lady's chamber of your heart . . . your conscience holds the key" (42). He also admonished her that she should guard against letting anyone else into her heart. In response to this revelation, Adelheid quoted directly from the Song of Songs, "Lord, if you have any love for me and care for me, then come to me yourself and send no messenger and kiss me with the kiss of your mouth" (42).

In imitation of *Song of Songs* 4, the Bride (Adelheid) and the Bridegroom (Christ) met in her locked and enclosed space where they could be alone together safe from any intrusion for she possessed the key (24). The Bride and the Bridegroom in the

Song of Songs professed love for one another. In the same way Christ and Adelheid professed love for each other. In each scene a fountain welled up in the midst of the garden as a symbol of life and of new life in Christ, that is—Divine Indwelling. Adelheid concluded her encounter with Christ in the garden professing the all-importance of Christ and ended with a direct quote (Cant. 1:2). "Lord, heaven is nothing to me, earth is too weak for me, the consolation of angels I count as nothing and I do not want the consolation of humans. Lord if you have any love for me and care for me, then come to me yourself and send no messenger and kiss me with the kiss of your mouth" (42).

The Use of Images from the Book of Revelation

Adelheid never directly quoted from the Book of Revelation, but her frequent use of images from that book shows an active knowledge of the biblical text. This was especially so when she portrayed Christ as the Lamb. While the nuns sang the *Sanctus* during Mass (a text already suggestive of the Book of Revelation 4:8) Adelheid heard the words, "Greetings from the Highest Lamb!" (17) She wished to know who that was and inquired, "I recognize from your words that it is you who is speaking to me. Who is the highest Lamb?" (17) She received assurance that it was Christ himself. Christ proceeded to explain why Adelheid had to suffer stating, "Often I send you suffering so that I can praise you in heaven." (17) The sentiment expressed in this same dialogue is reminiscent of Revelations 3:1 RSV): "Those whom I love, I reprove and chasten; so be zealous and repent."

Bridal imagery also relates to the "Wedding Feast of the Lamb" in the Book of Revelation: "'Hallelujah! For the Lord our God the Almighty reigns. Let us rejoice and exult and give him the glory, for the marriage of the Lamb has come, and his Bride has made herself ready; it was granted her to be clothed with fine linen, bright and pure'—for the fine linen is the righteous deeds of the saints" (Rev. 9:6-8 RSV). On three occasions Adelheid experienced episodes of mystical marriage with the Lamb. On the feast of the Three Kings during Mass while the choir chanted the *Agnus Dei* ("Lamb of God, who takes away the sins of the world, have mercy on us") Christ spoke to Adelheid after she had obeyed his command and shown herself to be conscious of the feelings of the other sisters: "I will make you my bride today so that I will never be separated from you. I will show you all the loyalty that a lover gives to the Beloved. I marry you so that I will always remain with you and I will do everything you wish" (19). One year later Christ reminded her of this marriage and noted the detail that he had led her through the nine choirs of angels on that occasion and that the entire heavenly host of angels and saints had found her pleasing, and all showered her with wedding gifts (32). On St. Matthias Day Christ "consummated" the marriage: "I will give you myself, because I can show you no more love with anything other than myself" (55). Once again he led her through the nine choirs of angels and promised Adelheid: "Then you will be crowned with the purity of your heart" (55) and "I will be yours forever . . ." (55).

Also the imagery of the city that Adelheid described after she had been led by *Spes* and *Caritas* on a difficult journey reminds one of the New Jerusalem in the Book of Revelation. Adelheid's description:

> When she [Adelheid] heard about his beauty, she became powerfully strong and in joy she came to the place where the Lord, her Beloved lived. All the gates were opened to them. With joy they entered the city. It was so wide that she could not see to its end. All the paths in the city were of pure gold. It was so high that they could see no roof above. The city was bathed in bright sunlight which was its roof. She saw a bed in the city that was decorated with green velvet. The virgins put her down on the bed. While she was lying on the bed she saw her Lord approaching and he was so beautiful that I had never really heard of his beauty since

he was a thousand times more beautiful. His face shone brightly and his light outshone the light that filled the city. He came up to me and his beauty shone into my heart and went through all my limbs" (72).

Saint John described the New Jerusalem in similar language and used like images: "And I saw the holy city, new Jerusalem, coming down out of heaven from God, prepared as a bride adorned for her husband" (Rev. 21:2 RSV). Adelheid herself identified with this image in her journey to the meeting place with her Beloved. She was the bride who was prepared and had to be accompanied to the bridal bed with the encouragement of *Spes* and *Caritas*. One of the seven angels showed John the "Bride, the wife of the Lamb" (Rev. 21:9) who was likewise the new Jerusalem, the "dwelling of God" (Rev. 21:3). The association of the city as the dwelling place of God and the constant refrain in the Book of Revelation that God dwelt within, link Adelheid (the Bride) and the city. When Adelheid asked Christ to show himself to her, he responded: "Look into your own heart!" (25). In a revelation Christ also admitted to Adelheid, "See, thus have you captured me in the lady's chamber of your heart" (42). He also professed to her, "Your heart is mine. I want to be in your heart" (62). The City, the Bride and the meeting place of Love exist within Adelheid. The City is the image of the fulfillment of love. The Bride shows the yearning and desire to share love. And the enclosed space makes it possible for Bride and Bridegroom to exchange their love for each other undisturbed.

The description of the City in both Adelheid's work and the scriptural text are similar. The New Jerusalem contains the "glory of God, its radiance like a most rare jewel, like a jasper, clear as crystal" (Rev. 21:11 RSV). It has "a great. high, wall" (Rev. 21:13 RSV) built from precious stones and each side has gates. However, the New Jerusalem has no temple, "for its temple is the Lord God the Almighty and the Lamb" (Rev. 21:22 RSV) and "the glory of God is its light, and its lamp is the Lamb" (Rev. 21:23 RSV). Only those whose names "are written in the Lamb's book of life" (Rev. 21:27 RSV) may enter it. The City contains the tree of life and its fruits (Rev. 22:2). Also, "the throne of God and the Lamb shall be in it, and his servants shall worship him; they shall see his face . . . (Rev. 22:3-4 RSV). Adelheid's description above was precisely the sort of imitation of imagery and themes that she had listened to in, for example, those readings in refectory. After describing a place similar to that recorded by Saint John, Adelheid embellished the setting making it a place of loving union, using erotic terms to emphasize the indwelling: "The Lord now approached the bed. In all his joyous beauty he knelt down before the bed and his face was turned toward mine. I looked up and gazed at him. He was so beautiful that I could not bear it and it seemed to me that my soul would dissolve from true love. He said, 'My Beloved!' With the same word that so sweetly came out from his mouth he drew my poor, sinful soul into his Godhead . . ." (72).

Adelheid mentioned specifically "the book of life" which is found seven times in the New Testament—once in Philippians (4:3) where Paul wrote of his fellow workers whose names were in the book of life, and six times in the Book of Revelation where the names written therein would not be blotted out (Rev. 3:5); while those whose names were not written in the Lamb's book of life would not be admitted (Rev. 21:27), but would be "thrown into the fire" (Rev. 20:15) because they had been judged by their deeds (Rev. 20:12) such as worshiping the beast (Rev. 13:8; 17:8). Adelheid's source was certainly the text from the Book of Revelation for she used the "book of life" especially in the context of Rev. 3:5. Christ announced to her on a Saturday at the beginning of Advent: "I want to write your name in the book of life so that it will never be erased from it" (15). Adelheid wished to know what is meant by this "book of life." In response Christ explained, "It is my divine heart that is the book of life. Whoever has been written down there can never be erased" (15). Adelheid also used this inscribing of the heart to apply to herself. "Lord inscribe your name in my heart so that it will never be erased." Just as her name would never be erased from his heart (the book of life) so his name would never be erased from her heart. This inscribing of the heart occurred at other times as well which emphasizes the union of Adelheid and Christ (33, 46).

Adelheid also alluded to certain experiences of St. Paul. She reported that on Candlemas she had to be led away from the table, being unaware that she was in the world. A flame shot out from her mouth and she exclaimed, "Lord God, have mercy on me!" (22). Immediately thereafter alone in her cell she asked the Lord where she had been. He told her, "Your soul was taken home to heaven and I cared for it and showed it to my mother" (22). Paul likewise described a similar incident. "I know a man in Christ who... was caught up to the third heaven—whether in the body or out of the body I do not know, God knows. And I know that this man was caught up into Paradise—whether in the body or out of the body, I do not know, God knows. And he heard things that cannot be told ... (2 Cor. 12:2-4 RSV). Also Adelheid, like Paul, had the choice of remaining on earth or going to heaven. Paul exclaimed, "I am hard-pressed between the two. My desire is to depart and be with Christ for that is far better" (Phil. 1:23 RSV). Once when Adelheid was gravely ill, Christ said to her, "If you wish to die now, I will grant you entrance into heaven, but you will have to relinquish the great reward that you could still gain" (29). Like Paul, who concluded, "... to remain in the flesh is more necessary on your account" (Phil. 1:24) Adelheid chose to remain among the living for the good that she could accomplish for others (29).

The Gospel of Luke and the Letters of Paul

In her *Prayer*, Adelheid quoted directly from the Gospel of Luke in German. In the *Prayer* she rehearsed events from the life of Christ and made reference to the incidents contained in Scripture, but she quoted directly three times from the scene of the Annunciation and once, in Latin, from Christ's baptism in the Jordan, "Hic est filius meus dilectus in quo mihi bene complacui" (138; Matt. 3:17 RSV: "This is my beloved Son with whom I am well pleased"). Since her *Prayer* rehearsed the major and often minor events from Christ's life, it alluded to all the Gospels and even to Pseudo-Gospels.

Adelheid's use of scriptural texts demonstrates knowledge of all four Gospels, St. Paul's Letters, the Song of Songs and the Book of Revelation. Her knowledge of these texts was both absorbed and practiced. It depended upon what she learned in singing the liturgical texts, listening to the refectory readings and chapel sermons, as well as pondering and reflecting on them to undertand better her own mystical experiences and the particulars of her relationship with Jesus.

CHAPTER FOUR

Literary Sources

In the now outdated critical edition of Adelheid's *Revelations* produced in 1878, Philipp Strauch referred to several literary influences, among which he made reference to *Das Hohelied* (ed. J. Haupt). In five instances he connected a paraphrase or image in the *Hohelied* with portions of Adelheid Langmann's *Revelations*. This *Hohelied*, published in 1864 at Vienna contains a German translation of the Song of Songs, Williram of Ebersberg's *Hohelied* written around 1060 as well as an extensive text interpreting the scriptural book written in the middle of the twelfth century attributed then to two abbesses of Hohenburg in Alsace—Rilindis and Herrat. More recently Friedrich Ohly asserts that the author is unknown. The correlations between this interpretive text, known as the *St. Trutperter Song of Songs*, and the *Revelations* of Adelheid Langmann occur not in the translated passages, but in their corresponding interpretations. According to Strauch, the Cistercian monks of Kaisheim, who frequently lent texts to the nuns of Engelthal, possessed a copy of Williram's *Hohelied*.[102] Whether this text corresponded to the Vienna manuscript (Hs. 2719) upon which Haupt based his edition remains uncertain. Nonetheless the textual correspondences suggest that Adelheid had the *St. Trutperter* text available to her in some form.

The interpretation offered by this text assumed various perspectives at different points. The first was a mariological interpretation.

Later the dialogue between bride and bridegroom is interpreted to be a conversation between the Church and the Synagogue. The author emphasized the role of the Holy Spirit coming to encounter the living God, which would also form an important element in the spirituality of Adelheid Langmann. Oddly enough the translation in Haupt's version began with a Latin scripture quote: "*Quia meliora sunt ubera tua uino flagrantia [sic] unguentis optimis*" (Cant. 1:1b-2a RSV: "For your love is better than wine, your anointing oils are fragrant, ...") rather than with the famous opening line of the Song of Songs used by Adelheid, "*Osculetur me osculo oris sui!*" (Cant. 1:1a RSV: "O that you would kiss me with the kisses of your mouth!"). However, prior to the beginning of the actual translation the author wrote at length on the kiss, describing the kiss between Virgin and Child:

> There was never a soul so lovingly kissed. The mouth with which she kissed was her will and her love. . . . He had kissed her before ever he spoke to her. He was the one who kissed, she the one he loved. She was the one kissed, he the one loved.[103]

In this mariological interpretation the author understood the kiss as a metaphor for the incarnation. Also, the kissing of the bride and groom symbolized Christ coming down from on high and taking on flesh from the humble Virgin.[104] Through this kiss (by becoming man) Christ kissed not only the Virgin, but kisses all human beings and offers them grace.[105]

Strauch saw an influence of Haupt 51:12f. on AL 85:26f (120) with regard to the mystical meaning of the gifts offered by the Three Kings to the Christ Child. Both interpret the incense as the prayers of the pure in heart. The use of the terms "drunkenness" and "Cyprian wine" to describe spiritual intoxication appeared in both AL 89:3 (140) and Haupt 25:1f. The most important connection noticed by Strauch concerns a quote identified in the *St. Trutperter*

Song of Songs with Saint Augustine. Adelheid recorded a revelation from Christ: "I will not be changed into you, rather you should be changed into me" (50).[106] This sentence clearly echoes the text under the commentary on Cant. 5:1b RSV: "Eat, O friends, and drink: drink deeply O lovers!" in the *St. Trutperter Song of Songs* which is attributed there to Augustine: "Not that I will be changed into you like food in your body, but rather you will be changed into me."[107] Here the greatest love is to eat the Lord (receive Communion). "Those who eat God are his friends," but his best friends are drunk on the immeasurable sweetness that they have with God.[108]

Other connections between the two texts beyond those mentioned by Strauch require a brief survey. The following passages may well have helped to form Adelheid's creative worldview since images, vocabulary and spiritual perspectives coincide. The most important element to note has to do with the role of the Holy Spirit. The *St. Trutperter Song of Songs* seems almost to be a commentary on the Holy Spirit for it begins, "We want to tell of the highest love, the greatest grace and the most fragrant sweetness: this is the Holy Spirit."[109] Throughout the commentary on the Song of Songs, the Holy Spirit plays a large role and receives extensive treatment especially at the conclusion of the work. Adelheid also stressed the importance of the Holy Spirit in the *Revelations*, more so than did her contemporaries such as Margaret Ebner. Since many of her visions and dreams were Trinitarian, the Holy Spirit naturally played a role in them. The Holy Spirit appeared in a revelation at Pentecost (24) and the teaching that he flowed out from the Father and the Son (25) connects Adelheid's revelation with the standard Latin position on the *filioque* controversy. In a vision on the feast of St. Peter the Preacher the Holy Spirit promised to bring Adelheid to perfection (32) and in a similar, but later vision the Holy Spirit promised, "I will never cease from granting her my goodness until she becomes the most perfect of all human beings"(48). In a subsequent vision the Spirit promised: "I give you all the virtues and I will confirm them in you" (51). On the feast of the Chair of St. Peter the promise was even more detailed, "I will make you so perfect with my divine goodness so that nothing will be lacking in you" (55). Adelheid prayed, "May you, Lord Holy Spirit, inflame me with the fire of your love so that my heart must burst more from love than from the pain of death" (95). For Adelheid the Holy Spirit was the driving force in the perfection of the soul in goodness and love.

Other elements that show Adelheid's use of the *St. Trutperter Song of Songs* have to do with vocabulary, symbols and the imaging of Adelheid's own history. Both texts utilized the term "martyrdom" of Christ to signify his passion. Symbolic adornment in which the colors or parts of vesture receive symbolic meaning appeared in both works. The symbolism of trees occurred in both texts. Adelheid may also have read her own history into the text of the *St. Trutperter Song of Songs* and used it in imaging her relationship with Christ. In the commentary on Cant. 8:6: "Set me as a seal upon your heart, as a seal upon your arm; for love is strong as death, jealousy is cruel as the grave. Its flashes are flashes of fire," Christ rehearsed what he had done for the soul. He created and saved it by his death. Speaking to Adelheid Christ said, "I drew you . . . against your will into my chamber (*kemenate*) onto the bed of spiritual suffering . . . so that you would love me above all things."[110] In this Adelheid read her own story for she likewise entered the monastery against her will and had to be induced to make profession (3-5). Adelheid specifically used the same word *kemenate* (a heated room) to signify the meeting place of lovers, of herself and Christ (42) and there in secret was told by Christ that he gives her suffering so that she will be his alone (8).

The Influence of Saint Bernard of Clairvaux

Saint Bernard of Clairvaux was a towering figure in his own time, Important as he was in political and religious affairs, all this is overshadowed by the lasting influence of his writings to which the spread of numerous copies of manuscripts produced all over Europe gives evidence. His influence extended not only to the wide circle of Cistercian and Benedictine monasticism, but to other monastics and religious as well. As an example of the lived experience of the mystical life in Christ and through his eloquent descriptions of the mystical life, he gained a lasting place in the hearts and minds of the Dominican nuns of the fourteenth century. For Adelheid Langmann his influence lay principally in the images as set forth in his famous sermons *On the Song of Songs*. Bernard wrote from the abundance of his meditation in *lectio divina*, but also from his experience, as he himself claimed, "I myself, however wretched I may be, have been occasionally privileged to sit at the feet of the Lord Jesus."[111] His inclusion of personal experience shows a new approach in interpretation. Although the biblical quotes and allusions that Adelheid employed might just as easily be said to have come directly from the Song of Songs, the spirit of their use and their interpretive context match Bernard's thought given in his sermons.

Saint Bernard of Clairvaux completed eighty-six sermons on the Song of Songs covering merely the first two of the eight chapters of the biblical text. He departed from earlier interpretations which saw the Song of Songs variously as a marriage song between Solomon and his bride, a conversation between the Church and the Synagogue, or a love song between Christ and his Bride, the Church. In his series of sermons Bernard personalized the text by interpreting it as a love song between Christ as Bridegroom and the believer as Bride. Every Christian soul, whether male or female, may enter into a bridal love relationship with Christ. In reference to the bride, Bernard posed the question, "Now who is this 'she'?" "She" is "the soul thirsting for God."[112] Under the influence of Saint Bernard when a Dominican, such as Adelheid, heard the Song of Songs or used it for *lectio divina* the interpretation and understanding of the text was at once personalized. Adelheid read about her own relationship with Christ in the text. The biblical passage and Bernard's interpretation helped her to make sense of her own experience. She was the Bride of Christ in a mystical and not simply in a metaphorical sense. What was true of the relationship and the progress of the biblical Bride applied also to Adelheid. Adelheid Langmann's spiritual progress mirrored the story of the Bride. Like the Bride, Adelheid was chosen by the Bridegroom, underwent trials of her love, was adorned with virtues so that she would become perfect and shared the marriage bed of the Beloved.

The social conventions of the writing of the Song of Songs made it necessary to assume that the Bride had been chosen by the Bridegroom. Adelheid, however, resisted Christ's choosing her to enter into a special relationship with him. Although, when still a young girl, everyone had said that she certainly belonged in a monastery, Adelheid refused to enter a cloister despite the revelations given to some other spiritual person about her and despite the assurances of others. Not until she had to deal personally with Christ's wish for her to enter the monastery of Engelthal did she reveal her apprehensions and ultimately acquiesced to the call. In her resistance to Christ she showed considerable theological acumen, if not actual casuistry, when she thought she would promise Christ whatever he wished, but be released from the vow by the priest because she would have made the promise against her will under duress. Ultimately Adelheid relented, convinced of the good will of Christ for her and assured of his assistance. Later she learned that her profession day had actually been a "wedding day" as were the profession days of all the nuns (10). Again and again Christ assured her that he would never abandon her and will never be separated from her, comparing their union with his immutable union with the Father (24, 25, 37). That Christ wrote Adelheid's name in the "book of life" assured her status as one of the elect (15). Explicitly Christ referred to her as his Bride and gave her gifts for their wedding. She could find Christ in her heart (25) just as she could be found in his (15). Adelheid's status surpassed that of all others, even Christina Ebner, and Christ spoke to her professing his love (42). His affections intensified, "I will be yours forever . . ." (55) and "I have chosen your heart for me . . ." (62). Finally, Christ using vocabulary reminiscent of *minnesang* told her: ". . . you are mine and I am yours. We are united and shall remain united forever" (63). He had chosen her to be one with him.

As the biblical Bride was tested by the Bridegroom (Cant. 3:1-2; 5:6-8) so Adelheid suffered tests of her love for Christ on several occasions. Aside from the initial disagreement over her vocation as a Dominican nun, Adelheid had to be taught the nature of the love that she must have for her Bridegroom. She had to give up her earthly family, but received the reward of membership in Christ's heavenly family (6). Also, she had to learn the purpose and the motive of suffering (7). Even though Adelheid suffered temptation by the devil (7, 71, 88), she also had assurance that she would grow in holiness (8). Making an analogy between Adelheid and the growth of a fruit tree, Christ taught her that she had a mission to help others (9). Christ told her that he sends her suffering so that he can praise her in heaven (17). On the feast of the Three Kings she proved both her obedience to Christ and her sensitivity to others, which prompted Christ to celebrate their marriage (19). On occasion Christ seemed disappointed in Adelheid's lack of response or her seemingly disloyal behavior. He wanted to know if she was ashamed of him (24). Christ asked her to "gladly bear suffering for my sake" (25) and reminded her of his own suffering for her. Christ commanded her to leave the infirmary although she was ill (26), requested that she eat the vegetables no matter how repulsive they seemed to her (27), allowed her to be frightened by snakes and vipers so that she would learn that "no one has received such great grace so as not to be on guard at all times against the wiles of the devil" (32). Adelheid also suffered from her own doubts, believing that the Lord will be unfaithful to her even as others were unfaithful and thinking that no one would do any good for her (37). Her doubts called forth reassurance and advice from Christ. Adelheid also learned of the exclusivity of her relationship with her Beloved when he upbraided her for a budding relationship with the Dominican preacher (43). She is admonished to come to

Christ for advice and consolation, and not to the preacher. Christ also exclaimed, after Adelheid had doubted the reality of a vision on Christmas, "How little you believe and how much it takes to make you believe" (50). Further, he warned her, "I will not be changed into you, rather you should be changed into me" (50). Adelheid must also give gifts—her soul and body, and all human beings whom she has ever met (51). Her final test had to do with Christ's plan to betroth Adelheid to St. John the Evangelist. Despite her feeling of rejection, she proved that she would do his will (52).

Just as the Bride in the Song of Songs was adorned with ornaments, jewels and gold so Adelheid was adorned with virtues so that she would grow in holiness (Cant. 1:9-11). Throughout the Song of Songs the Bride's anatomy, clothing and raiment are described. Any anagogical or allegorical interpretation of the biblical text would attach symbolic significance to the description of the Bride whose physical beauty and rich attire reveal the inner beauty of the soul and its adornment with virtues.

This imagery connecting virtues with garments or crowns occurred often in Saint Bernard's sermons and appeared in Adelheid's writings as well. Writing of the Bride, Bernard noted the "splendor of her adornment" as far surpassing the raiment of Solomon.[113] She was "graced with the jewels of consummate virtue" which were "more brilliant than the sun."[114] The Bride's beauty consisted in virtues: love, justice, patience, voluntary poverty, humility, holy fear, prudence, temperance, and fortitude. This virtue and clothing symbolism Adelheid employs in her *Revelations*. On the feast of the Holy Trinity Christ gave her three different colored garments and explained their symbolism. When Adelheid asked what the white dress signified, he responded: "It symbolizes true purity since I have purified you of all your sins. The red dress signifies the burning love that you have for me. The green dress signifies my divinity for I am within you" (11). He then placed a crown upon her head which should be decorated with the jewels of her good deeds. Christ restored the garment of innocence to her and professed that she was dearer to him than any other human being on earth (25). He promised to do whatever she wished and on numerous occasions professed that he would never be parted from her (24, 25, 37, etc.). Much to Adelheid's chagrin, Christ took a virtue from every sister in the monastery and gave them to her instead (29). When Adelheid finally demonstrated that her will was in total accord with Christ's, she received promises and gifts from God the Father, the Holy Spirit, the Virgin Mary, and the archangel Gabriel (32). On a second occasion through the intercession of the Virgin Mary the members of the heavenly company made promises to her. From God the Father she received divine power to resist all vices. Christ gave her divine wisdom. The Holy Spirit promised to make her perfect (48), by giving her all the virtues (51). Ultimately Christ conferred upon Adelheid what amounted to a new baptism:

> "My Love, it is necessary for me to wash you all over. First, your eyes so that they will look at me alone and also your ears so that they will hear my teaching and the teachings of my teachers so that you will keep them; and your nose so that it will detect the falsehood of the world and know that faithfulness is found in no one, but me alone. Your heart should belong to me alone and have no one except me. Your tongue should speak the truth for it should rightly be that those who do not speak the truth should have their tongues ripped out. Your mouth should praise me at all times. Your hands should do my works. Your feet should walk in my ways. You should gladly come to me. All the strength of your limbs should be consumed in my service. I have purchased heaven for you by my death. You must serve me . . . I have given my life for your sake and am dead for you and you must give your strength for the kingdom of heaven . . ." (56).

This imitated the blessings at baptism with the sanctification of various body parts by anointing with oil or by being touched in some way—the head, the breast, the tongue, the ears (*ephphetha*) etc. In poetic language Christ promised to give Adelheid a share in the love of the patriarchs, the confessors and the virgins (62). Her new baptismal identity and beginning destined her to join the company of these saintly and faithful witnesses.

As the biblical Bride was perfected by association with the Bridegroom so frequently did Christ promise that he would make Adelheid perfect. Ultimately the biblical Bride is led into the wilderness of her Beloved, and is sealed with love that is as strong as death (Cant. 8:5-7). These three verses represent the climax of the entire poem and can be interpreted to symbolize union and therefore perfection in love between the Bride and the Beloved. With regard to Adelheid the Holy Spirit had also promised, "She cannot reach perfection without me. I want to bring her to perfection" (32). Christ reiterated what he had done for Adelheid and promised, "I shall never let up with my divine power until you have become a perfect human being" (35). On another occasion the Spirit promised, "I will never cease from granting her my goodness until she becomes the most perfect of all human beings" (48). This promise was repeated later, "I will make you so perfect with my divine goodness that nothing will be lacking in you" (55). The call of the sacrament of baptism to make it possible for the Christian to become holy is fortified by the sacrament of matrimony which destines the husband and wife to become holy precisely as a married couple. The Trinity made Adelheid capable of becoming holy by baptism and Christ, as her Bridegroom helped her to fulfill her destiny of being holy in the sight of God and others.

Although her marriage to Christ was mentioned on several occasions with reference to her profession (a new monastic "baptism" (16) and to her marriage (19) on the octave of the Dedication of the Church (41), it was in Christ's bedchamber to which she had been led by *Spes* and *Caritas* that Adelheid experienced the ecstatic consummation of union (72). For Saint Bernard, " . . . the bedroom [represented] the mystery of divine contemplation."[115] There in the bedroom of contemplation God "is neither fearsome nor awe-inspiring, he wills to be found there in the guise of love, calm and peaceful, gracious and meek, filled with mercy for all who gaze on him."[116] Adelheid had previously prayed to be united with Christ: "Lord, unite yourself to me and me to you so that our union will last forever without any separation" (24). The amazing revelations during the sermon of the unnamed Dominican preacher (40-42) foreshadowed the consummation of the marriage with Christ in that the lovers both professed their love in unmistakable terms (42). Christ spoke to her in loving words, "My Beloved, sweet as sugar or honey, my Tender One, my Pure One, you are mine and I am yours" (63). And when she prayed for the knight of Hohenstein, Christ revealed to her, "With this man I will let you know how much I really love you (70). By her advice and prayers the knight became a Cistercian monk, something which he had not foreseen. The climax of her bridal relationship with Christ occurred in the vision where she was led by *Spes* and *Caritas* to the wedding bed.

> The Lord now approached the bed. In all his joyous beauty he knelt down before the bed and his face was turned toward mine. I looked up and gazed at him. He was so beautiful that I could not bear it and it seemed to me that my soul would dissolve from true love. He said, "Beloved!" With the same word that so sweetly came out from his mouth he drew my poor, sinful soul into his Godhead and I can say nothing about this vision except to say that it began when they had begun to sing compline and continued until the next day as Mass was being sung (72).

Adelheid wrote specifically about the "kiss of the mouth" in response to the incredible blessings she had received in the revelation during the preaching of the Dominican.

> Lord, heaven is nothing to me, earth is too weak for me, the consolation of angels I count as nothing and I do not want

the consolation of humans. Lord, if you have any love for me and care for me, then come to me yourself and send no messenger and kiss me with the kiss of your mouth (42).

This concluding request found an echo in Bernard's sermons: "... if he has genuine regard for me, let him kiss me with the kiss of his mouth."[117] To understand the fullness of meaning behind that expression one must know the depth of meaning given to it by Bernard of Clairvaux. He devoted three sermons (2,3,4) to an interpretation of "O that you would kiss me with the kisses of your mouth" (Cant. 1:2). He differentiated three types of kiss: the feet, the hands and the mouth of Christ. The kiss of the feet was a sign of genuine conversion of life. When describing this kiss he wrote of the penitence and love of Mary Magdalene: "It is up to you, wretched sinner, to humble yourself as this happy penitent [Mary Magdalene] did so that you may be rid of your wretchedness. Prostrate yourself on the ground, take hold of his feet, soothe them with kisses, sprinkle them with your tears and so wash not them but yourself."[118] As a symbol of reconciliation the kiss of the feet was also a sign of peace, as are all the kisses.[119] When Adelheid described the kiss of the feet she treated each foot separately. From the right foot she should draw out divine faithfulness and from the left, divine purity and protection from evil (81). These corresponded to Bernard's "genuine conversion of life" in that both faith and purity were required for conversion. Mary Magdalene had turned away from a life of sin and had put her faith in Jesus. Adelheid followed her example.

Saint Bernard's "kiss of the hands" was given to those who are making spiritual progress. The kiss of the hands represented the reception of grace.[120] God's grace was necessary for perseverance in conversion. Adelheid, again, separated the kiss between the two hands. From the right hand she should draw divine mercy and from the left, obedience (81). For her, these were the tools of perseverance. She had to learn to obey Christ's commands to her and to conform her will to his under all circumstances. To do this she begged for God's grace and mercy especially in her own *Prayer* (94).

Adelheid also mentioned the kiss of the side of Christ from which she would receive the abundance of the divinity and humanity of Christ (81). Although she prayed to receive the "kiss of the mouth" explicitly in her *Revelations* she did not treat of it using those terms, however, this kiss of the side of Christ bore some of the meaning attributed to the kiss of the mouth by Bernard, for his "kiss of the mouth was no other than the Mediator between God and man, himself a man, Christ Jesus, who with the Father and Holy Spirit lives and reigns as God for ever and ever. Amen."[121] Both Christ's humanity and divinity were contained in each kiss. Bernard further described the "kiss of the mouth" in Trinitarian terms:

> Listen if you will know what the kiss of the mouth is: 'The Father and I are one;' and again: 'I am in the Father and the Father is in me.' This is a kiss from mouth to mouth, beyond the claim of any creature. It is a kiss of love and peace, but of the love which is beyond all knowledge, and that peace which is so much greater than we can understand. The truth is that the things that no eye has seen, and no ear heard, things beyond the mind of man, were revealed to Paul by God through his Spirit, that is, through him who is the kiss of his mouth.[122]

Saint Bernard quoted or paraphrased verses from scripture here: 'The Father and I are one' (John 10:30); 'I am in the Father and the Father is in me' (John 14:10); 'love which is beyond all knowledge' (Eph. 3:10); 'peace which is greater than we can understand' (Phil. 4:7); and 'no eye has seen . . .' (1 Cor. 2:9). The progression of types of kisses climaxes in the ineffable experience of mystical union in love, peace and mystery.

In imitating Bernard Adelheid was greatly influenced by Trinitarian spirituality. In many of her visions, the Trinity of

Persons played a major role (25, 48, 76 etc.). Adelheid desired the kiss of the mouth for it symbolized union with Christ and, in fact, with the whole Trinity through him. She described this union in her vision of Christ's bedchamber in which their union was consummated (72). Bernard also described the kiss in Trinitarian terms: "If, as is properly understood, the Father is he who kisses, the Son he who is kissed, then it cannot be wrong to see in the kiss the Holy Spirit, for he is the imperturbable peace of the Father and the Son, their unshakable bond, their undivided love, their indivisible unity."[123] Christ often promised Adelheid that just as little as he could be separated from his Father, would he be separated from her (24, 25, 37).

Textual Correspondences: Bernard and Adelheid

There are also numerous correspondences of texts which suggest the influence of Bernard on Adelheid. These range from descriptive detail about angels to statements concerning the virtues of the Bride or the Bride's capability to behold the beauty of heaven. These correspondences occur frequently throughout the text of the *Revelations* and in Adelheid's *Prayer*. I shall treat only a few of the more pertinent parallels in the texts.

On one occasion Adelheid, having been roused from ecstasy, desired to know where she had been. It seemed puzzling to her to learn from Christ that she had visited heaven, but could remember nothing. She asked him, "Lord, why did you not let me know it?" and he responded, "You are not yet worthy of it, but it will happen to you soon" (22). The Bride in Bernard's sermon heard similar words explaining why she could not see heaven. "The vision that you ask for, Bride of mine, is above your capacity, you are not yet able to gaze upon that sublime noontide brightness that is my dwelling place."[124] In the same sermon the Bridegroom consoled the Bride using words from the biblical text that occur frequently in Adelheid's *Revelations*. "The time will come when I shall reveal myself and your beauty will be complete, just as my beauty is complete you will be so like me that you will see me as I am. Then you will be told: 'You are all fair my love, there is no flaw in you.'"[125] The Holy Spirit promised Adelheid, "I will make you so perfect with my divine goodness that nothing will be lacking in you" (55). In her *Prayer* Adelheid made a petition to that same end: "And so I ask you to bring me to all perfection and fill me up with all graces so that nothing will be lacking in me and you will find me ready at all times when you come" (98). The same phrase applied to Christ when he made the very claim for himself, "There is nothing lacking in me" (43). Adelheid's thought matched the teaching of Bernard. Just as Christ was perfect (nothing lacking) so Adelheid would be made perfect, but for now she was not yet able to see heaven.

The unity in love between Bride and Bridegroom and between Adelheid and Christ was expressed in similar words in the *Revelations* and in the sermons *On the Song of Songs*. Bernard's Bride exclaimed, "My Beloved is mine and I am his!"[126] Christ likewise used this formula to express his love for Adelheid: "You are mine and I am yours!" (63).

The Divine Indwelling

Saint Bernard's comments on the indwelling of Christ in the heart found a reflection in Adelheid's *Revelations*. Bernard taught that Christ dwells in the virtuous as in heaven.[127] His supporting scriptural quotes also suggest Adelheid's experience. "Christ dwells by faith in our hearts" (Eph. 3:17) corresponds to Adelheid's relation of how Christ told her to look into her own heart to find him (25). In this regard Bernard also quoted from the Gospel of John, "I and the Father will come to him and make our dwelling with him" (John 14:23).[128] The mutuality of the indwelling mentioned by Bernard found a powerful resonance in Adelheid. Bernard expressed this mutual union in the following way. "Therefore, when God and man cleave wholly to each other — it is when they are incorporated into each other by mutual love that they cleave wholly to each other—I would say beyond all doubt that God is in man and man in God."[129] Adelheid used "pressing" instead of Bernard's "cleaving" to express the same reality. Christ promised Adelheid, "I will press your soul to my divinity so that you will be as like me as is possible" (55). Later, he "stretched out his arms, embraced her and pressed her against his divine heart so that she thought she clung to him like wax to a seal" (76). The writing of the Name of Jesus in her heart also symbolized their union, but even more importantly Christ wished to write his name on her heart as a testimony of mutual love and the coincidence of wills (33). The unity of the two occurred for Bernard and for Adelheid in the unity of wills. Bernard wrote, "But that unity is caused not so much by the identity of essences as by the concurrence of wills."[130] As we have seen Adelheid had to be trained to unite her will with the will Christ for her.

The Influence of Mechthild of Magdeburg

If Margarethe Weinhandl's claim that Mechthild of Magdeburg influenced the thought, images and vocabulary of all middle and South German mystics rings true, then this certainly applies to Adelheid Langmann.[131] Other scholars noticed similarities in narrative detail, imagery and vocabulary between Mechthild's *The Flowing Light of the Godhead* and Adelheid Langmann's *Revelations*. Philipp Strauch noted five instances of concurrence between the writings of the two mystics. More recently Siegfried Ringler has also emphasized the importance of the mystic of Magdeburg on the spirituality of the monastery at Engelthal. In all likelihood the bridge between Mechthild and the nuns of Engelthal was Henry of Nördlingen. Henry either translated Mechthild's *The Flowing Light of the Godhead* or had someone else translate it into an Alemmanic dialect making the text more easily readable by southern German nuns. Mechthild's book survives only in this translation. When Henry of Nörlingen corresponded with Margaret Ebner, a nun and mystic at Maria Medingen, he interspersed the text with "lengthy quotes from Mechthild of Magdeburg's *The Flowing Light of the Godhead*.[132] From his self-imposed exile in Basel, Henry sent the nuns of Medingen a copy of Mechthild's book calling it "the most interiorly moving shot of love, that I have ever read in the German language."[133] Henry recommended the text to Margaret (and possibly to the nuns of Engelthal) to help her make sense of her mystical experiences. He also mentioned this book as belonging to the monastery of Kaisheim, the prior of which conducted correspondence with Adelheid Langmann (156-159).[134] In Letter XLIII, Henry also wrote that he wished to send the book to Engelthal.[135] Apparently he also corresponded with Christina Ebner of Engelthal.[136] Knowledge of, and correspondence among various nuns including Christina and Margaret Ebner seems evident since Henry mentioned friendship between them and directed Margaret to write to Christina.[137] Henry visited Engelthal for at least three weeks in 1351 and probably had the same kind of connection with that monastery as he did with Maria Medingen being well known throughout southern Germany for his preaching and spiritual direction.[138] Quite probably then, according to this external evidence, Mechthild of Magdeburg's *The Flowing Light of the Godhead* influenced the writing of Adelheid Langmann through the connection of Henry of Nördlingen, Ulrich of Kaisheim, the nuns of Maria Medingen and the Dominicans of Engelthal.

Internal textual evidence likewise supports the claim that such influence existed. This evidence consists principally in various common episodes, imagery and vocabulary used in the texts. Philipp Strauch pointed out a connection with regard to Adelheid Langmann's vision of the Christ Child and the host during the celebration of Mass (30) and similar accounts in Christina Ebner's *Revelations* and Mechthild's book.[139] Adelheid reported her vision:

[D]uring the Gospel Our Lord appeared on the altar in the form of a little child. He jumped down and ran over to all his friends and consoled them. When the priest began the preface, the child jumped back upon the altar and as the priest elevated the host, the child was changed into the host, but when he should receive the host, the host changed back into a child who resisted with his hands and feet. But when he received the host, his heart became as bright as the sun and the child played within him. When the priest gave the blessing, the child leapt over to the sister and grew larger to about the age of four and embraced her and kissed her and then ran over to the altar and back again and embraced and kissed her once again" (30).

Mechthild reported a similar incident when a priest was celebrating Mass: "When he took the white hosts into his hands, the same lamb which had been standing on the altar arose and, when he said the words and made the gestures it changed into the host and the host became the lamb, so that I no longer saw the host, but only a bleeding lamb hanging from a bloody cross."[140] Both Mechthild and Adelheid reported visions concerning the Eucharist, a not uncommon phenomenon among medieval mystics.

Strauch also noted that according to Dionysius the Carthusian in his *Colloquium sive Dialogus de particulari iudicio animarum post mortem* (1614), Mechthild of Magdeburg shared in the belief that there were souls in purgatory who had completed their penance, but who nonetheless remained in purgatory. Mechthild wrote of three heavens, the second of which may correspond to Adelheid's experience (91). "The second heaven is made from the holy longing of the senses and from the first degree of love. In this heaven there is no light, and the soul cannot see God. She tastes an ineffable sweetness which flows through all parts of her body."[141] Margarethe Weinhandl also compared Adelheid's vision of purgatory (91) with that of Mechthild.[142] Adelheid's was less descriptive and was concerned only with the uppermost part of that place of purification where souls had already done penance, but were denied the vision of God. Adelheid experienced their pain and described it as an unquenchable thirst for God, for the vision of God and for the one Hail Mary necessary to deliver those souls from purgatory into God's presence. With Mechthild this description was more detailed: "Thereafter, through help and forbearance they pass beyond all distress. This is so close to heaven that they possess all the joys but three: They do not see God. They have not yet received their honor. They have not yet been crowned."[143]

Strauch noted as well the formulaic use of a phrase from the anonymous poem *"Du bist min, ich bin din"* (You are mine, I am yours). Adelheid wrote, ". . . you are mine and I am yours. We are united and shall remain united forever" (63). Mechthild expressed the same sentiments when she wrote, "I am in you and you are in Me."[144]

Similar expressions for the computation of time appeared in both works. Both Mechthild and Adelheid measured time according the length of a prayer. "Truly I cannot bear to think about it for as long as it takes to recite the Hail Mary."[145] Adelheid spoke of a period of silence lasting the length of fifty *Ave Marias* (70).

Other passages from Mechthild, not previously noted by scholars, also find a resonance in Adelheid's *Revelations*. Book Three, Chapter One, may portray the kernel of the episode Adelheid described when she was accompanied by *Spes* and *Caritas* to the bridal bed of Christ. In Mechthild' version two angels accompanied the soul to bring her home. Despite still being "clothed with the dark earth," she [the soul] wished to ascend to her love."[146] They (the two angels) took the soul between them and led her joyfully away."[147] When she had arrived in the land of the angels her Beloved, "looked into her face. Note how she was kissed there. With this kiss she was raised to the highest heights above all the choirs of angels."[148] In Adelheid Langmann's vision love-sickness weighed her down when *Spes* and *Caritas* came to her and asked why she was so ill. Like Mechthild's soul, she yearned for her Beloved, but feared that he would not come to her because of the heaviness of her sins (72). *Spes* and *Caritas* sang the praises of Christ's merciful love and encouraged Adelheid to make the journey to meet the Beloved. After faltering twice they spurred her on by asking her to meditate upon the beauty of the face of her Beloved. They concluded their argument saying, "All that is beautiful in heaven and on earth is nothing when compared to his beauty. Joy beyond all joys have those who look upon him forever" (72). Finally they brought her to the dwelling place of the Beloved, described in terms similar to those used to describe the heavenly Jerusalem. The Beloved approached her bed. His beautiful face gazed into hers so that it seemed to her that her "soul would dissolve from true love" (72).

Both Mechthild and Adelheid gave prominence to the role of the Holy Trinity in their works, perhaps more so than Adelheid's contemporaries. Regarding the characteristics and activities of God there are further correspondences between the works of Mechthild and Adelheid. The mystics shared spiritual worldviews and made use of the same images and vocabulary. The importance of the wine cellar as a mystic symbol and the corresponding description of the drunkenness of Christ or the Bride to indicate an intense spiritual experience found expression in both works (141).[149] Both mystics employed clothing symbolism connecting various colored garments (11, 80), crowns or jewels with virtues (11, 55, 61, 80). Both wrote frequently of the nine choirs of angels (29, 32, 55, 87).[150] A more detailed study into the similarities between Mechthild and Adelheid's works would also include the image of "flowing from the Trinity," "love-sickness," "flower/tree symbolism," the "wounds of Christ," the "kiss," and the *Gnadenfrucht Topos* (the fruits of grace topos) in which the mystic is promised deliverance of a certain number of souls from purgatory or strengthening in faith for lukewarm souls or confirmation in faith for those who already believe firmly.

CHAPTER FIVE

Manuscripts and Texts

The monastic life within the Dominican cloister of Engelthal nurtured the flowering of an intense mysticism in the fourteenth century which led the nuns to experience the mystical presence of God in an immediate and personal way. This development in turn inspired Dominican nuns in other monasteries, formed the character of mystical preaching among Dominican friars and other priests, and presented to the Friends of God confirmation of the Christian ideal of holiness of life. The intensity and duration of mystical experiences among so many of the nuns compelled them and their chaplains to record the events in various forms so that others might know the wonders of God and be encouraged in living out an authentic Christian life. From this treasury of texts at Engelthal come the autobiography of Christina Ebner called the *Revelations*, or *Das Büchlein von der Gnaden Überlast*, the *Sister-Book* of Engelthal, in which Christina recorded the lives and mystical experiences of the nuns who came before her in the community; *The Life of Sister Gertrud of Engelthal; The Life of Grace of Friedrich Sunder*; and the autobiographical *Revelations* of Adelheid Langmann. The richness of texts testifies to the intensity of religious life at Engelthal and the receptivity of the nuns and those associated with them to strive for personal and powerful contact with Christ. It also shows the desire and willingness to record these experiences for the welfare and edification of others.

Adelheid Langmann's *Revelations* fulfills an important part in the construction of a distinctive mystical spirituality at Engelthal.[151] As the autobiography of an ecstatic mystic it takes a major place among the documents produced at Engelthal because it reports the personal experiences and theological vision of one individual.

Manuscipt M

Manuscript M (=Munich) is kept at the Staatsbibliothek in Munich (Cgm. 99). The text appears on pages 36-173, having been bound at a later date with works by Jan van Ruysbroeck. Adelheid's text follows its own pagination in Roman numerals. This manuscript bears no title and remains unfinished since the red capital letters which indicate new paragraphs as they appear in this translation have not yet been filled in from page 165b to the end. At the beginning of the manuscript the scribe carefully plotted the lines so that they would be even and straight with fifteen lines to the page. Later there is no evidence of such care and the number of lines per page varies between fourteen and nineteen lines. After page 118 the scribe seems to exhibit new care in copying the text, but soon relaxes, making unwanted marks on the page. However, numerous marginal notes indicate an effort at completing scribal omissions to correct the text after different sections had been completed. Manuscript M appears to be a copy of an earlier version.

Manuscript B

Manuscript B (=Berlin), originally belonging to the Monastery of St. Katharine in Nuremberg, is now in the possession of the Staatsbibliothek Preußischer Kulturbesitz in Berlin (mgq. 866). The text was written in two hands (1. pp. 86v-88; 105-215; and 2. 89-215) and was bound together with other texts copied in a hand from the fourteenth and fifteenth centuries and was finished according to a note on page 310, "completus est liber iste XXI junio 1404" (this book was completed 21 July 1404). A third hand on p. 86v. made the following notation: "Anno Domini MCCC or more in the city of Nuremberg there was an honorable family named Langmann who were related to the Ebners. From them was born a child who was called Adelheid. What wonders God did with her from her childhood and the Holy Spirit worked through her, you will presently hear. Whatever was seemly, praiseworthy, spiritual or godly, the child had and was indeed happy among people without being fresh."

Both manuscripts are written in Bavarian with a strong admixture of a Middle German dialect.[152] Other than that the two texts have considerable differences in content, chronology and length. Strauch based his critical edition published in 1878 on M and B, preferring the Berlin manuscript, but always noting the differences and distinctive features of the Munich manuscript.

The Berlin Manuscript is longer than M. It contains a lengthy prayer attributed to Adelheid Langmann (94-155) and the letter exchange with Ulrich of the Monastery of Kaisheim interwoven into the text (156-162) and the episode in the school (23). However M also has texts not found in B: Eckhart of Hohenstein's first communion (70), the death of Elsbet (79) etc. Also various episodes appear in different places in the sequence of events, i.e. the temptation by devils on the night before profession of her vows (88) appears in M immediately before the account of the day of profession (14), whereas in B it is reported much later in the sequence of the text.

Manuscript W

A later edition of the *Revelations* of Adelheid Langmann, unknown to Strauch when he prepared his critical edition, is the *Codex Scotensis Vindobonensis* 308 (234) at the Bibliothek des Schottenstifts in Vienna. In his detailed analysis of the manuscripts Siegfried Ringler designates this edited text as W (=Wien) and asserts that this version differs to a greater degree from M and B than they do from each other. However with regard to texts deleted or added to B it agrees with M. W is a paper manuscript completed in 1451 with an epilogue appended in 1457.[153] The manuscript consists of 238 pages written by a single hand in a clear *Bastarda* from the fifteenth century. On page 229r the scribe identifies himself as Hans Probst. The descriptive epilogue telling how the manuscript found its way to the monastery of St. Katharine was written by Anna Jack. The number of lines per page varies between 25 and 34 and rubrics were used throughout to indicate Latin quotations, names, underlines etc. Originally the manuscript belonged to the Franciscan monastery of Inzigkoven. Aside from the works having to do with Engelthal, this manuscript contains numerous other spiritual texts by Gertrude the Great of Helfta, Marquard of Lindau, Gregory the Great and Henry of Louvain. It also includes monastery chronicles of Kirchberg and another unnamed monastery in the vicinity of Ulm, and numerous other devotional texts. This version is the shortest of the three, omitting single words, abbreviating, reformulating sentence structure and using passages in an entirely different way. The scribe intentionally abbreviated the text in order to tighten the reports by eliminating repetitions and facts known in general.[154] W usually omits names, titles, descriptive details and epithets such as "holy" and "divine." This tendency to abbreviate can be demonstrated especially in references to Christ and the Virgin Mary. Manuscript M typically refers to Christ as "unser lieber herre"; whereas Manuscript B has "unser herre" and Manuscript W often replaces that with "er." The same pattern occurs with references to Mary: M "unser liebe fraue," B "unser fraue," M usually agrees with B. Altogether W abbreviates passages in fifty instances. More importantly, Ringler theorized that the editor abbreviated many passages because of objectionable content. Among these are statements about the lack of faith of Adelheid (12) [AL 7:25-8:16], her sucking from the wounds of Christ (77) [AL 67:33-68:3], and the numbering of individuals saved from purgatory, sinners converted or believers strengthened in faith through the prayers of Adelheid or as a gift from Christ. This pattern called the *Gnadenfrucht Topos* occurs fifteen times). All of these passages are omitted or abbreviated because they throw doubt on the faith of Adelheid or contain erotic language or images.[155] However the major difference of this version, according to Ringler, is the addition of an introductory paragraph and a brief conclusion. The introductory paragraph in W agrees in content with the marginal note contained in M. The content of the conclusion of M is the same as that of W. I agree with Ringler that these additions to the text show a strong tendency to historicize the text and to direct it and make it amenable to an audience. However such a tendency, as interesting and as well-intentioned as it may be, removes the text from the autobiographical and places another level of interpretation between the author and any audience. Such an interpretation as exhibited in W while seeking to enlighten or explain the text directed to a new audience may just as easily obscure or falsify the text. It is my belief that the "naughty bits" or embarrassing passages intentionally eliminated in W because they do not conform to some preconceived notion of what religious life should be, must be included precisely because they throw the reader back into the realm of wonder or mystery and thereby emphasize the reality that God works in mysterious ways and that he deals with human beings according to human nature. The relationship between God and any mystic is a private affair. The course of events, the attitudes, the graces and the interpretation by the individual mystic demonstrate the way that God related to one individual. To read such an autobiography offers entry into a privileged experience of a relationship, it does not necessarily teach a lesson applicable to the reader, nor invite the reader to imitate the same experiences. While I agree with Siefried Ringler's thesis that the progression of manuscripts shows a *Legendarisierungsprozess*, a progressive process of formulating a legend in the sense of an edifying work for the benefit of the reader, I intend to offer in this translation a complete text of the *Revelations* of Adelheid Langmann in the autobiographical rather than legendary form, in so far as this is possible given the state of the manuscripts. Of greatest importance for achieving this is Manuscript B. Although, as Ringler noted, it was hastily written, it contains Adelheid's *Prayer* and the letters from the prior of Kaisheim and prefers first person narrative. Aside from that, it belonged originally to the monastery of St. Katharine, a daughter house of Engelthal. These facts indicate a more authentic text. Manuscript M rearranges large episodes, has numerous variations, seeks a unified style of reporting, and prefers a third person narrative. Manuscript W imposes a chronological framework with introduction and epilogue similar to those in the Munich Manuscript and abbreviates the text extensively and especially because of content. In preparing his critical edition of 1878, Philipp Strauch rightly favored the Berlin Manuscript. With this translation I also favor Manuscript B, while noting the subsequent redactional changes in the other manuscripts.

The Translations

Although manuscript B includes all three works, the *Revelations*, the *Prayer*, and the *Letters*, and presents them as one document, here I shall discuss each as an independent unit. Manuscript M and W do contain neither the letters nor Adelheid's *Prayer* either by omission or by their addition to B. In the Berlin manuscript, as in this translation, the *Prayer* begins after (93) and serves as a mystical climax of the autobiography. There was no attempt to integrate the *Prayer* into the text of the *Revelations* since it does form an independent unit. However, at the conclusion of the *Prayer* the autobiographical narrative of the manuscript commences again (156) without any title to mark the beginning of a new section. The three letters were then clumsily tacked onto the main narrative. While care was taken to preserve these vestiges of Adelheid's correspondence it would have been better to title this part of the manuscript and to separate it clearly from the autobiography.

The Revelations (1-93)

The similarities and differences in the manuscripts have been discussed above. In the present translation I have incorporated all the texts from each manuscript within the framework of manuscript B, which Strauch and Ringler consider to be the closest to the original writings of Adelheid. I chose to place the introductions and conclusions from M and W in the notes because they represent obvious additions to and clarifications of the original text, not written by Adelheid herself.

The text of the *Revelations* began with the sign of the cross in Latin and as such Adelheid invokes the Holy Trinity. That Adelheid chose to begin her autobiography in this way indicates three interpretive possibilities: *Revelations* as document, prayer or sermon.

Many public documents of the time began by invoking the Trinity. Since Adelheid composed her *Revelations* only under obedience, this beginning may indicate her awareness that these events of her private relationships with heavenly and earthly personages will be made a matter of public knowledge. This "official" beginning implies that her private experiences are worthy of being recorded and revealed for the edification of others.

The Trinitarian opening may also indicate the prayerful content of the document to follow. The *Revelations* is an autobiography of a nun whose concerns and interests were primarily spiritual in kind. She recorded the many events of her relationship to God and noted their impact on her life and thought. Consequently very little detail concerns secular or family matters. Adelheid understood her life and sought to portray it as a document of grace under the care of the Trinity. Her life-story functions as a prayer for in it she recorded the remarkable events of temptation and grace which led her to rise to her special status as beloved of God. She heard the Gospel preached and loved it, and indeed everyone (except her family) thought she should become a nun (1). Despite the family's matchmaking, Christ powerfully arranged that she should be his for he had chosen her for himself (3). Because of advice from spiritual friends and by these revelations from Christ, Adelheid overcame her real reluctance to entering a monastery caused by fear of the harshness of the monastic regimen (5). She reported diabolic temptations (7) and divine revelations (8, 9).

The *Revelations* may also be interpreted as having the qualities of a sermon for these would typically begin with the sign of the cross invoking the Trinity, and could well end with an "Amen." The author announces the theme in the first paragraph. This "sermon" tells about the action of God in the life of Adelheid Langmann to show what wonders God worked with her and to teach that the Holy Spirit came to dwell within her. As such the text reports not only the autobiographical details of Adelheid Langmann's relationship to Christ, but also edifies the reader, who will understand the importance of this relationship and hope for the marvelous attitude and actions of Christ to be present in all believers.

The Prayer (94-155)

Adelheid Langmann's *Prayer* consists of sixty-one petitions addressed to the Holy Trinity. It serves as a *summa* in brief of her personal theological vision expressed through the prayer concerns of each petition and through the progression of petitions as a whole. Each petition has a two-fold structure beginning with the proclamation or rehearsal ("I remind you . . . .") of some event in the course of salvation history. Each petition concludes with the request that either some attribute stemming from that event be given to Adelheid (or to those for whom she intercedes) or some personal benefit may come through the power of that salvific event from the life of Christ. Each petition makes Adelheid present to the personage or moment invoked. She addresses the Trinity, the Godhead, the Father and Christ as she rehearses significant moments in history touched by divine intervention. She calls to mind events before time began as well as the episodes of the private and public life of Jesus up to the institution of the

Eucharist at the Last Supper. The *Prayer* as extant may very well be incomplete. There seems to be no definitive end to the prayer and the expectation that Adelheid should continue in the same manner by including the events of the passion, death and resurrection of Christ and perhaps even the post-resurrection events such as Pentecost and Ascension, is strong. Perhaps the rest of the prayer has been lost. It may also be that Adelheid composed a separate and perhaps somewhat different prayer designed for meditation on the passion events. That would not be unusual given the predilection of fourteenth-century mystics to contemplate the sufferings of Christ in minute and explicit detail. Given Adelheid's theological perspective, I doubt that such a prayer exists, but if it did it would undoubtedly resemble her vision in (72) where she asserted that love was the motive for all of Christ's sufferings, and repeated the love motive in response to every action of Christ's public ministry and to every act of suffering Christ endured. However, I argue that the *Prayer*, as contained in manuscript B and in this translation, has an integrity of its own in that it expresses Adelheid's theological vision and can be interpreted as a single and complete unit.

The *Prayer* can be understood as a summary of Adelheid's theology and the opening paragraph functions as a synopsis of the *Prayer*. Not surprisingly, Adelheid addressed the prayer to the Holy Trinity. Unlike her contemporary Dominican mystics whose spiritual focus was directed toward Christ and particularly toward him crucified, Adelheid's spirituality was Trinitarian. In her *Prayer* the passion of Christ in the events of Good Friday disappeared from consideration. She thought of Christ in a much broader context beginning with his presence in the Eternal Trinity and ending with his coming in glory at the end of time to judge the living and the dead. Adelheid's theological vision co-extends with eternity. In this largest of contexts everything and everyone has its place and its meaning and contributes to the progression of salvation history under God's providence.

Most importantly, in her *Prayer* Adelheid interpreted her own place within the scope of providential history. She prayed to become the mouthpiece through which all the cries and yearnings of every human being before her time would be channeled. Their prayers for love and mercy would be collected in her and uttered through her own mouth before the Triune God. It is as if she understood herself to be Queen Esther for the whole human race. In the same breath she prayed that all the cries and yearnings of every human being from her own day to the end of the world would be channeled through her. "They must all come forth from my mouth . . ." (94). Adelheid assumed the Christological function of priestly intercession to herself. As intercessor she stood in a long line of powerful figures who interceded in behalf of others. Abraham wagered for the just men of Sodom (Gen. 18:22-33). Moses lifted up his hands in prayer for victory while Joshua and the Israelites waged battle with Amalek (Exod. 17:8-13). Queen Esther pleaded the cause of the endangered Israelites before King Ahasuerus (Est. 15). All of these righteous individuals made intercession in behalf of a distinct group of people under particular circumstances during a specific period of time. Adelheid's intercession far exceeds that of each of these biblical personages, in fact, her intercessory prayer resembles that of Christ himself. Just as Jesus died for all for the forgiveness of sins, so Adelheid pleaded for all to receive mercy and love. Christ's motive for dying was love for all. Adelheid prayed that his mercy and love be extended to everyone who has ever called out for it. She called forth the motive and the historical action of the crucifixion into the personal and real lives of all people. What the Trinity intended (salvation for all), and Christ accomplished by his obedience and crucifixion (the possibility of and invitation to salvation) Adelheid prayed to happen in reality, not simply in theology or intention. She prayed for others and she also prayed for herself what she would wish for others. God should come into her heart and fill her with love and grace, remove her sins and make it possible for her to lead a holy and perfect life so that she would be found perfect on the last day (94). With this first petition she prayed for the accomplishment of salvation within her. Her concept of salvation cannot be minimalized. She conceived of salvation for her and for the whole world as the union of God and herself in her heart. She would be totally transformed and would be set apart as holy and therefore become godlike. Further she would become completely divinized in "perfection." Such a process would complete the saving work of Christ in Adelheid and therefore would make his sacrifice fruitful in her.

Repeatedly Adelheid prayed for this divinization to be accomplished in her by asking for "perfection" (98), or for a "holy and perfect life" (94); for graces "so that nothing will be lacking" (98) in her, for being made "holy in real truth" (104); and for being "found perfect" at her death (148). Adelheid conceived of this progress toward human perfection as a gift of God's grace which would gradually and continually provide her with the virtues necessary to lead a life transformed by the divine presence. To foster this process she prayed for "perfect humility" (101) and "all virtues" (100) so she would be able to benefit from God's free gift. With regard to faith she also asked to "know the truth" and even to have hidden mysteries revealed to her just as had happened with the Virgin Mary. Most importantly she asked for mercy and love suspecting that Christ operated according to the same motive for individuals as he had for the world when he offered up his life on the cross. Emphatically, Adelheid prayed twice to receive such love from God that her "heart must burst more from love than from the pain of death" (95, 134). She associated Christ with herself in two ways: as her Beloved or Bridegroom (95) and as her "child" who would be "born spiritually within" her (106). The first image links her with bridal mysticism (*Brautmystik*) and the second alludes to essence mysticism (*Wesenmystik*) thus linking in one prayer and spirituality two contrasting symbol systems, both of which sought to describe the indescribable immediate relation of God and the soul.

The reception of the Eucharist functioned as the prime image of the reception or conception of Christ within Adelheid. The indwelling of the divine now motivated no longer by love for the world, but by love for Adelheid individually brought to bear the benefits of the salvific acts of Christ in his life and on the Hill of Calvary to Adelheid herself. The indwelling of Christ, like reception of the Eucharist, brought forgiveness of sins, illumination to truth, and spiritual growth fostered by love. With such an understanding, it is not surprising that Adelheid concluded her *Prayer* with the institution of the Eucharist on Holy Thursday and its application to her and effect upon her. "I ask you to give me true, perfect love to receive your Holy Body so that I may conceive you spiritually even as your mother conceived you bodily . . ." (155).

The Letters (156-161)

After the *Prayer* following a break in the text of Manuscript B the *Revelations* continues with the addition of possibly six letters worked into a redacted narrative. It was done in a clumsy way and would have been greatly improved by inserting the complete text of each of the letters which would have clearly indicated each letter in its integrity. However, as the letters appear in the text, it is difficult to interpret them, impossible to date them or to determine whether the text contains three or more letters from Ulrich of Kaisheim to Adelheid. Wilhelm Oehl included and designated the texts as Letter 1 (159), Letter 2 (160) and Letter 3 (161), but did not include the text of (156, 157, 158) which could be excerpts from as many as three different letters.[156]

By comparison to Ulrich's five extant letters to Margaret Ebner, the letters to Adelheid seem more spiritual in content. Perhaps if the extant text included the greeting to each letter, they would more closely match the style of the letters to Margaret. In writing to Margaret, Ulrich passes on greetings and news in response to Margaret's inquiries, but never discusses any spiritual topic. In fact he refrains from doing so writing that he will discuss some matter known only to Margaret when he comes to visit her at the monastery of Maria Medingen.[157] The matter seems to be too important or private to be included in a letter. Kaisheim was much closer in location to Margaret Ebner's monastery than to Engelthal making it easier for Ulrich and Margaret to speak of important concerns in person, while Adelheid would have had to rely on letters to communicate matters which would have preferably been discussed in private.

The letter fragments do reveal the spiritual closeness of the nun Adelheid and the abbot Ulrich. Their relationship seems to have been one of mutual confidence and trust. Each one depended upon the other for intercessory prayer and prophetic revelations. Both exhibited bridal mystic tendencies, and emphasized the importance of the Holy Trinity in the spiritual life. They united bridal mysticism and Trinitarian spirituality in the indwelling in the heart. In that way neither would ever be separated from God or from one other. Ulrich wrote of Christ being "drunk" with love for Adelheid and emphasized her role as intercessor for all because she was able to obtain anything she wished from her bridegroom. In addition to the bridal imagery, Ulrich also wrote of the birth of the Christ Child in the soul, a very popular idea among the German mystics. In response to his letter Adelheid, using first person, recorded that she did not understand that very will (162). However, a revelation to her clarified the result of the birth of Christ in the soul—Adelheid would receive power to convert sinners to goodness, the task for which Christ took on flesh, preached and died. In the final revelation, Christ proclaimed that, "... no one can do anything more dear to me than to pray for sinners" (162). For Adelheid, to be united with Christ and to accomplish the same conversion of sinners was her lifework.

PART TWO

Texts

The *Revelations* of Adelheid Langmann

1. In the Name of the Father and of the Son and of the Holy Spirit I begin this account of the life of a cloistered nun showing how God displayed wonders to her from the days of her childhood and how the Holy Spirit dwelt within her.[158] Whatever seemed proper and pleasing in spiritual and divine matters this child performed and she appeared happy to all without being boisterous. Whenever she went with her mother to hear the preaching she listened well and locked the message in the interior of her heart.[159] Then when she came home and was alone she pondered the words of the sermon and especially liked to meditate upon the martyrdom of Our Lord according to her understanding.[160] The people who were with the child and took care of her soon noticed this. They often said to her mother, "The child certainly belongs in a monastery."

2. This was how things stood until the girl reached the age of thirteen years. Then she was engaged by her relatives to a young man, who, however, was mortally ill. When the wedding should have taken place and while she was sitting in the bridal chair the young man had to take to his bed the whole day. His illness grew worse until he died the next year.[161]

3. Afterward her relatives wanted to arrange another marriage. Then Our Lord spoke to someone: "If they were to find thirty bridegrooms, all of them would have to die. She must be mine." Then she asked good people to pray for her to recognize God's dearest

will. While praying, a good person asked God whether it was his will for her to enter a monastery. Then Our Lord said, "Yes, it is my will. I want to have her where she will be one with me." Then the person asked, "Lord, where will she be one with you?" Then Our Lord said, "Where she is no one."

4. After that on the feast of the Apostles Philip and James, this same person prayed for her to the holy apostles saying, "Much beloved saints, today I wish that you would pray to Our Lord for this woman to know if it is his will that she enter a monastery."[162] Then the saints said, "Yes, it is his will that she follow after us, the saints, and that she, like us, should give up her own will." Then the person asked, "Lord, what will you give her for doing this?" Our Lord answered, "At her death I will give her the heavenly kingdom."

5. Now this young widow had the custom of taking the discipline seven times every day whenever she wished according to her need.[163] Once at Christmas after she had received Our Lord in communion and had the host in her mouth, it was so strongly stuck against the roof of her mouth that she could not consume it. Even when she took a drink it did not help. Then she thought to herself, "Dearest Lord, what have I done against your good grace?" Then in her mouth the Lord himself said to her, "You have done nothing against me. If you should promise me that you will enter the monastery of Engelthal, you will receive me." Then she said, "Lord, I will not do that. I am too sick and do not want to endure evil." Then Our Lord said, "Then you will not receive me." She thought to herself that she should tell this to the priest so that he might help her. Then Our Lord answered her thoughts, "Neither the priest nor anyone in this church can help you to receive me unless you promise me." Then she thought that she would promise and that the priest would release her from it because she would have made it against her will. And once again the Lord answered her thoughts saying, "That is also not my will. I want you to take the vows, even if you should die in fulfilling them." Then she thought, "Lord, I shall take the vows even if I should die." And immediately she received him. She

said, "Lord, today I have given you my will and my young body. Will I become holy in the monastery?" He said, "Yes, because I will never leave you and I myself will help you out of all the suffering you will ever have and I want to do good to you as my most beloved and will never separate myself from you." Immediately Our Lord removed all desire for transitory things from her and she was truly joyful to be entering a monastery. Nevertheless she thought about her family with a heavy heart because she would have to leave them.

6. Afterward, fourteen days before Easter, this woman received Our Lord. And when she had received him she offered him all her family saying, "Lord, today I entrust my whole family to you and I shall never be concerned about their lives or goods." Then Our Lord said, "So I shall make you forget your family. Turn to my mother and to all my saints as your intercessors before me." After that none of her family remained loyal to her for they would rather have seen her stay in the world. Now it happened that her family sought her out twice in order to get her to marry against her will. Then she left their sight and was never seen by them again. They took all her possessions away.

7. As this woman was traveling towards her monastery she came by a church. She asked to be admitted for a while and when she entered she fell to her knees before the crucifix and asked Our Lord to relieve her from the deep sorrow that she bore. When she looked up she saw Our Lord hanging on the cross with bleeding wounds. He said, "See how much I have suffered for your sake. And you can not endure so little for my sake? I will relieve your suffering." Then she continued on to her monastery where she lived for a time without any consolation from the Lord. The devil tormented her every night with intolerable pain. He dragged in corpses and laid them in her arms. He brought her an axe and a hatchet.[164] All night he bellowed like an ox so that she found no rest in sleep. One night he came to her and sat down on her bed as if he were her aunt. Then she asked, "Are you my aunt?[165] He kept silent. Then she recognized him, raised up her hand and blessed

herself. He mocked her. This condition continued one year in the world and a year in the monastery.

8. On the first Holy Thursday after she had entered the monastery, when she went to receive Our Lord, he forgave her all her sins and said to her, "You should grow green like the trees and you should bear fruit as well as leaves." She did not understand these words, but she dared not ask him to explain. He gave her thirty-thousand souls from purgatory and just as many sinners to be converted and the same number of devout people to be confirmed in faith. Then she had a failing that caused her sorrow. She said, "Oh Lord, what do you intend with this suffering?" Then Our Lord answered her saying, "Had I not given you such suffering, you would have taken up too much time with others. But you are ashamed before them and must remain with me and you will learn that they are not faithful." However, Our Lord promised her that he would free her from her affliction.

9. One day she wanted ardently to know what Our Lord had meant when he said, "You should grow green like the trees." Then Our Lord came to her and said, "Do you not understand that? You should grow green like the trees in virtue and should bring forth fruit as well as leaves. When the trees bloom, first the leaves appear and among them the blossoms. But when the petals fall the fruit appears. You should blossom and bring forth fruit and I will pick you. Many people will be converted through you. You are my child. You are my sister. You are my bride. I am your father because I have created you. I am your brother because I became man. I am your bridegroom because I have chosen you."

10. One time when a child was received into the same monastery the nun cried during the *Veni Creator Spiritus* and thought about the suffering that she endured when she had been admitted.[166] Then Our Lord came to her and said, "Today is the child's wedding day. Should I also wed you?" Then the sister asked, "Was there a wedding here when I was admitted?" Our Lord answered, "I myself was here with my mother and my twelve apostles and my

martyrs and confessors and the eleven-thousand virgins.[167] On that very day many saints and angels earnestly interceded before me for you so that I would make you good. They said, you had invited them." Then the nun said, "That is true. I visited as many churches as I could and invited them all to come." She asked, "Were you also gracious on that day?" Our Lord said, "Truly, whatever you asked me for, I gave you. And whoever prayed to me for your sake, I answered the prayer." She said, "Lord, was any soul saved?" He said, "Indeed, thirty-thousand souls were freed from bondage and as many sinners were converted and just as many devout believers were confirmed in their faith. If you had asked me for all the souls in purgatory I would have given them to you. But for so many you were unable to pray. I helped you put on your habit. That you had to dress yourself without the help of anyone else is a sign of this. Isn't that true?"[168] She answered, "Yes, Lord, many people know that." Our Lord said, "My mother and I accompanied you and went with you through the choir to all the nuns. And I rejoiced that you had been made worthy of me." She continued to ask whether the child would also become good. Then he said she would be cleansed of much and become good.

11. One time on the feast of the Holy Trinity during the *Agnus Dei* this sister fervently prayed that Our Lord would come to her.[169] Then Our Lord came and said, "Peace be with you! I, the Father in heaven, love you." Then the Son said, "I love you too!" And the Holy Spirit: "I, the true Godhead, love you!" She asked Our Lord to dress her. Then he said, "I shall do that." He clothed her in a white garment, then a red and then a green one and said, "I have dressed you." She asked, "Lord, what does the white dress mean?" He answered, "It symbolizes true purity since I have purified you of all your sins. The red dress signifies the burning love that you have for me. The green dress signifies my divinity for I am within you.[170] Now I have placed a crown on your head. The crown has five-thousand settings in which are set little precious stones." She asked, "What is that from?" He answered, "Your good deeds should

fill them up." She prayed to him for the souls in purgatory. He gave her fifteen-thousand souls and as many sinners were converted and just as many devout people were confirmed in the faith. He said, "If people knew how great this day is, they would serve me more eagerly than they do now." The sister felt so well in the presence of Our Lord that she said, "Lord, let me always be with you. I desire no other heaven." Then he said, "Peace be with you" and went his way.[171]

12. One time after Mass this sister was meditating on the passion of Our Lord. When she came to the point when he hung on the cross, she heard, "Peace be with you always." She asked, "Who are you and why are you speaking to me?" Then he said, "I am the true God and true Man who rose on Easter day and then ascended into heaven." Then this sister began to cry and said, "Oh dear Lord, now I hear so many tell how the evil spirit tricks people and if I should lose my reward, it would have been better if you had never created me." Then Our Lord spoke, "I swear to you by my divine power that I am your God and Lord." Then she thought to herself, "Oh, if only you were speaking the truth." Then he swore it again. Then she thought to herself, "If only you would let yourself be seen, I would believe." Immediately Our Lord appeared before her as an old man whose face was wonderfully beautiful, but still appeared angry. As soon as she saw him, he entered her heart and asked, "Now do you believe that it is I?" She answered, "Yes, Lord, I do believe." Then he said to her, "I give you no good other than divine good and offer no grace other than divine grace. Now believe me. Peace be with you!" Then he disappeared. From then on she believed that he would do good to her.

13. One time on the feast of the Assumption of Our Lady, she received Our Lord.[172] The Lord gave her one-hundred-thousand souls, an equal number of sinners and the same number of good people to be strengthened in faith. Then she wished that this would also happen to someone else. And so it did. It happened to someone four miles away, who came and told her about it.

14. When it came time for this sister to make profession Our Lord asked her to make a general confession. He wanted to give her another guardian angel. She promised the Lord that she would do it.[173] [88. During the night before the day when she should make her profession many devils came and brought a wagon and said, "Come with us! You should go to hell with us! You do not belong in the kingdom of heaven!" Then she said, "Away with you, you evil wretches! I trust in my Lord Jesus Christ. He will never let me be parted from him." Then they screamed so loudly and made such a noise that she became very ill from it and she could not utter another word, thinking she would die from such distress. So little strength was left in her that she could not lift her hand to make the sign of the cross. So she formed a cross in her mouth with her tongue. She thought to herself, "If only I could cry out, I would call out so that people would come to me." After that she thought, "No, Lord, I swear that if you wish it of me I will suffer this up to my death. But only do not leave me!" Immediately after that she lost consciousness. Then angels came ever closer to her and many of them played harps, but most of them blew shawms.[174] The holy angels drove the devils away. The angels floated up to the windows in the cloister and were as bright as the sun and they played their shawms and their playing was sweeter than any music she had ever heard. She went into the chapter room and in the prioress' place sat a lord who wore the most beautiful attire. It went beyond what one could imagine. The color resembled the daffodils in May.[175] On the cloth sparkled innumerable little golden stars and his face shone like the sun. She knelt down before him and he received her vows. When she had promised him obedience, he embraced her in his arms and enclosed her in his cloak and pressed her lovingly against his heart and said, "May you be well, my beloved child, and do not fear for I will never abandon you." And she believed him to be her dear lord, St. Dominic.] On that same day she received Our Lord and took her vows. Once again Our Lord forgave her all her sins and said, "I shall never separate myself from you, neither now

nor hereafter." She said, "Oh Lord, since I am so sick, how will I ever carry out the observances of my Order?" He answered again, "Fulfill your vows happily. Whatever you are unable to do, I will do. I will never abandon you in any need of body or soul." She prayed to him for souls and reminded him of his promise. Then he gave her twenty-five-thousand souls and the same number of sinners and the same number of good people to be strengthened in faith. And he gave her another angel and commended her enthusiastically to the angel. The angel said he would gladly watch over her. Our Lord commended the angel to her and said she should be happy to pray to him since he is a princely angel. She asked him why he had given her another angel. Then Our Lord answered, "You have entered into a higher calling and I have given you an angel of higher rank since you will have need of him. A king has a higher angel than a duke—the higher the person, the higher the angel."

15. One Saturday at the beginning of Advent at vesper time this sister cried bitterly and implored Our Lord to come down to her from heaven just as he had done so graciously before. Our Lord came to her and said, "Peace be with you!" He said many things to her that she has since forgotten, but especially he told her, "I want to write your name in the book of life so that it will never be erased from it. With that farewell!"[176] She asked, "Lord, what is the book of life?" He answered, "It is my divine heart that is the book of life. Whoever has been written down there can never be erased." Throughout this Advent he never left this sister without giving her special consolation.

16. On the Sunday before Christmas the nuns were eating the evening meal so late that candles had to be lit. Then this sister thought to herself, "Oh Lord, candles are usually lit at a wedding feast when it gets so late. Which one here will be the bride today?" She continued thinking to herself, "Oh if only in your goodness, you would make me your bride." Then a candle was lit in front of her so she thought, "Yes, indeed, I am the bride." Then Our Lord came to her and showed her so much kindness that she could scarcely get

up from the table. She had to be led to her cell. There she burst out laughing loudly and conversed with Our Lord. Because of him all was well with her. This lasted until Mass and he was her benefactor and gave her so much joy that she forgot all the suffering she had already had to endure. Then she had no control over herself and could no longer speak.

17. Afterward on Christmas day when she received Our Lord, it seemed to her that Our Lord had not favored her as much as before. She began to cry bitterly. And on other days during the Mass she cried and said, "Lord, I will not stop crying until you come to me." During the *Sanctus* Our Lord came to her and spoke kindly and full of love beyond all measure. "Greetings from the highest Lamb!" Then she thought to herself, "I recognize from your words that it is you who is speaking to me. Who is the highest Lamb?" He answered, "I am the highest Lamb. I myself have greeted you. Why are you crying, my Beloved? Whatever you wish, I also wish. Your burning tears drew me down to you from heaven. I have come and will take away your tears with me back to heaven and will show them to my heavenly Father and my mother and all the saints, so that they will love you even more and will not begrudge all the good I will do for you. Often I send you suffering so that I can praise you in heaven."[177]

18. Then after Mass on the feast of the Holy Innocents Our Lord came to this sister and was gracious to her.[178] She asked him about her family. He promised her that none of them would ever be separated from him. When she asked about any of her relatives or friends, he would tell how it would turn out with them. Then he gave her four-thousand poor souls and as many sinners and good people to be strengthened in faith.

19. After that during Mass on the feast of the Three Kings she desired Our Lord with all her heart.[179] During the *Agnus Dei* Our Lord came and gave her good things and remained with her until she heard the bell to go to table. Then she said, "Lord, give me your blessing since I must go to table." "You should stay here. I give

you permission." Then she said, "I know that well, but still I fear annoyance from the others." He said, "If you do not stay here, I will not give you anything good and you will also not have permission." So she stayed there gladly. Our Lord said, "Because you wanted to leave me to avoid annoyance to the others, but still remained here, I will give you the same reward as if you had read the psalter sixty times. I will make you my bride today so that I will never be separated from you. I will show you all the loyalty that a lover gives to the Beloved. I marry you today so that I will always remain with you and I will do everything that you wish. I will commend you to my mother and my saints so that they will be good to you." Then Our Lady said to her, "Be assured, my dear child, I will be good to you." The sister said, "Oh dear Lady, do not treat me like a wicked mother-in-law with her apron strings." Our Lady said, "I will not treat you as a wicked mother-in-law with her apron strings. I will take care of you like a faithful mother would care for her child. Whenever my Son is angry with you, I will reconcile you." Our Lord said, "Ask me for whatever you will, I will grant it." She said, "Lord, you know well that whenever a lord celebrates a wedding feast in his castle, he has the right to free all the prisoners. Now you are a Lord above all other lords and therefore show mercy today to the prisoners." Our Lord said, "Ask me for whatever you wish. If you were to ask me for all the souls in purgatory I would give them to you." She said, "Lord, you should give me them yourself. Young brides do not like to ask. Whatever is given to them they take." He said, "Take sixty-thousand souls today and just as many sinners that I want to convert and just as many devout people that I want to strengthen in faith."

20. This sister was so beside herself that she did not know what to do. Then St. Nicholas appeared dressed as a bishop and gave her the Body of Our Lord. Then she came to herself again and remembered that a bishop had given her Our Lord. However, she did not know who he was. Then Our Lord said, "That was St. Nicholas and this happened to strengthen you. Every bridegroom gives a wedding band, so I have married you by giving you my body."

21. Then on the eve of Candlemas at vespers this sister thought to herself, "Oh dear Lord, take me to yourself!"[180] Then she was so sad that she thought she would die and said, "Lord, let me stay here so that I will gain more reward." The nuns led her behind the altar, and when she looked up the choir was filled with light and Our Lord said to her, "If you had continued thinking that you wanted to die I would have taken you with me to heaven." She said, "Lord, if it were your will, you would have given it to me." The nuns led her out of the choir to the bed in her cell. After she had rested they brought her something to drink. Then she said, "Ever since I entered the monastery, I have never drunk undiluted wine." Then those who attended her said, "It is not undiluted wine, but mixed according to the custom." And they drank with her. Then they said, "We brought mixed wine, but this is undiluted wine."

22. On Candlemas as they went to table, she had to be led away again.[181] She lay there the whole day until vespers unaware of being in the world. But as night fell she went to table and had to be led away again. When they had brought her into the corridor she cried out with a loud voice, "Lord God, have mercy on me!" Then a flame shot out of her mouth. She was led into her cell. Then Our Lord came to her full of grace. She said, "Lord, where have I been today? I know for certain that I was taken away, but I do not know where." Then Our Lord said, "Your soul was taken home to heaven and I cared for it and showed it to my mother. She showed it to the whole heavenly host and you were very pleasing to all of them." She said, "Lord, why did you not let me know it?" Then Our Lord said, "You are not yet worthy of it, but it will happen to you soon."

67. [182]One day the nanny who raised her came to the monastery. Then the sisters went to her and asked her about the child and said, "Tell us, dear Kunigunde, have you ever experienced anything special about her? Then she answered, "Yes, one day as I sat by the cradle leaning on it I fell asleep. Then the most beautiful lady that my eyes have ever seen came and she had on a blue mantle. And this mantle was so wide that if it had ever been unfolded it would

have covered the whole world.[183] She said to me, 'Kunigunde, are you sleeping?' And she woke me up. Then I said, 'Not I, Madam!' So she asked me three times whether I was sleeping and each time I answered, 'Not I, Madam!' Then she said, 'May this child be entrusted to you. Be good to her and I will reward you. Know that she will become a good person and many sinners will be converted through her.' Then I asked, 'Lady, who are you?' Then she said, 'I am the Mother of Mercy.' And as soon as she had said that I never saw her again. Indeed my heart was so filled with grace that I was happier taking better care of the child than before. Once at night a light shone above the cradle. It was more brilliant than sunshine and was so bright that I could not bear it. Then I picked up the cradle with the child in it and ran out of the room. Then everyone who was in the house said to me, 'Kunigunde, what are you doing?' Then I said, 'A light came from heaven and wanted to take the child from me and the light was so bright that I was blinded by it.'"

23. [184]One time she received Our Lord in school. After eating she was doing arithmetic and everything went blank. Then Our Lord came and learned in her place and showed her his great goodness. The next morning the teacher asked her, "Where were you yesterday?" She answered, "I was here learning." Then the teacher asked, "Did Our Lord learn or did you?" Then she pleaded with her teacher never to speak of this. From then on she was better able to count.

24. At Pentecost in the year of Our Lord 1330, this sister received Our Lord and when she had received him, it seemed to her she was encircled by fire.[185] She said, "Lord, unite yourself to me and me to you so that our union will last forever without any separation." Our Lord said, "Just as little as I can ever be separated from my Father, so little will I ever be separated from you. I have also given the Holy Spirit to you just as I gave him to my apostles." Then she saw the Holy Spirit in tongues of fire. He gave her thirty-thousand souls from purgatory and as many repentant sinners and just as many devout people confirmed in faith. He asked, "Why do you

not profess me? Are you ashamed of me? I am helpful enough to you. I profess you before my Father and my saints and will never deny you. You should love no one as much as me. If there were a duke, who had a poor maiden who took up with an evil servant instead, the duke could well say, "I am not suited to you." Then that evening Our Lord sent her such grace that she could move neither her hands nor her feet.

25. One day later the sister desired Our Lord again during Mass. Then Our Lord came during the *Sanctus*. She asked him to give her the kind of life that would always keep her closest to him. Our Lord said, "I have already restored to you the garment of innocence that had been given to you at baptism.[186] You are dearer to me than any other human being on earth. I, the Father, love you and so does the Son, who proceeded from my heart and yet remains forever with me, and also the Holy Spirit, who flowed out from both of us and who remains eternally in us." She said, "Oh Lord, yesterday you said that you had given me the Holy Spirit just as you had given him to the apostles. But they knew all languages and everything I do not know." Our Lord said, "Your soul received me just as they had and it knows everything that they knew. If the need were there, then I would give it to you so that it would overflow from your soul into your body. Now it is not necessary. Your soul knows everything that they knew. And if the entire heavenly host begged me to withdraw my divine grace from you, I would never withdraw it because I love you so much. You would have to do much evil against me to incur such a punishment." She said, "Dearly beloved Lord, for the sake of the love that you showed me yesterday, let me see you." He said, "Look into your own heart!" She looked into her heart and then she saw her soul sitting across from the Lord. Her soul said, "Oh Lord, stay with me forever and give my body something to do so that it will perform holy works so that you will never be parted from me." Our Lord said, "I will do that. As little as I can separate myself from my heavenly Father, so little do I want to separate myself from you." Then her soul bowed down before Our Lord and

he put his arm around her. After she lay there awhile, he asked her to stand up. She said, "Lord, inscribe your name on my heart so that it will never be erased." He said, "I will do that." Then he raised his right hand and wrote the name "Jesus" on her heart. Four of the letters were in gold. The "E" was red.[187] She said, "Lord, write my name on your heart also!" He said, "I will do that." The Father and the Son and the Holy Spirit were present. What joy and grace there was then, no one would be able to tell. Our Lord said, "Ask me for whatever you will, I will give it to you." She asked him for many things. He said, "It is granted." She saw him there with his five wounds and sharp swords, just as he would sit in judgment on the Last Day.[188] He said, "Gladly bear suffering for my sake. See what I have suffered for you."

26. After that on the feast of the Holy Trinity she was in the infirmary.[189] Then he urged her to leave the infirmary. She said, "Oh Lord, you know well how very sick I am such that I think that my soul will leave my body." He said, "Now pay attention. I will make you strong." And further, "People go to the infirmary and begin to talk. You should leave it so that I can do good things for you. I give you permission. The prioress is standing at the altar." She looked up. There at the altar stood the prioress. She left the infirmary and went into the refectory. Then Our Lord was good to her beyond all measure.

27. Once the vegetables tasted so bad that she did not want to eat them. Then Our Lord came to her at table and said, "Beloved, eat the vegetables for my sake." She answered, "Oh Lord, I would rather cry than eat this." Then he said, "Well begin to eat. I will give you five-thousand poor souls from purgatory." Then she ate them all up and would gladly have eaten more they were so good.

28. On the feast of St. John after Easter the sister cried a great deal and yearned for the joy of heaven.[190] Then she saw the open wound full of blood on the side of Our Lord. She understood this to have come from love and that also he wanted to hear her prayer to take her away.

29. Seven days later she became sick and received Our Lord in the infirmary. And when she received him, Our Lord said to her, "If you wish to die now, I will grant you entrance into heaven, but you will have to relinquish the great reward that you could still gain." She said, "Lord, then let me live longer and earn greater reward." Since she had given her own will over to God she was so outside of herself that she no longer understood anything about the world. That continued until the Mass was sung and all the sisters had received the Lord. Then she came to herself again. She said, "Dearest Lord, I know well that you have given me great grace, but I do not know what kind." Then Our Lord said, "You desire to be in the monastery. So I took your soul into my arms and carried it through the monastery and from every sister I took what pleased me most about her and gave it to your soul so that it would be that much more beautifully clothed and therefore appeal to me even more." Then the sister thought, "Oh Lord, if anyone were to take something from me and give it to another it would cause me grief." Then Our Lord said, "To many who prayed to me for you I granted their wish. Many have saddened you and have not made up for it. You yourself prayed for the monastery and because of that I heaped graces upon you from my friends. And when I had adorned your soul with them I led it through the nine choirs of angels." Then the sister said, "Oh dear Lord, was I pleasing to them?" Then Our Lord answered, "They all liked you very much and all praised you."

30. One day when the sisters received Our Lord, this sister asked the Lord fervently to grant this to her. The next day when the Mass of Our Lady was being sung she thought to herself that she must be so displeasing to Our Lord that he did not want to grant her wish, but during the sequence she was in ecstasy and during the Gospel Our Lord appeared on the altar in the form of a little child. He jumped down and ran over to all his friends and consoled them. When the priest began the preface, the child jumped back on the altar and as the priest elevated the host, the child was changed into the host, but when he [the priest] should receive the host, the

host changed back into a child who resisted with his hands and feet. But when he received the host, his heart became as bright as the sun and the child played within him. When the priest gave the blessing, the child leapt over to the sister and grew larger to about the age of four and embraced her and kissed her and then ran over to the altar and back again and embraced and kissed her once again. Then she turned away and resisted his kisses thinking to herself, "Perhaps you are not Our Lord after all." Then he showed her his hands and feet and side and said, "Now believe that it is I." She said, "Lord, forgive me and give me your blessing." Then he raised his right hand and made the sign of the cross over her and said, "Peace be with you," and disappeared.

31. On Easter in the year of Our Lord 1331, this sister received Our Lord.[191] Then Our Lord forgave all her sins and granted her thirty-thousand souls from purgatory and just as many sinners for conversion and again as many devout people to strengthen in faith. He said to her, "Today I receive you into the company of all my friends, among whom you have not yet lived. From now on and forever, whenever anyone thinks of good people, you will be among them." From that same Easter day until Pentecost no day passed without Our Lord granting her some special gift.

32. Once Our Lord had promised to wed this sister. Then during the Mass on the vigil of St. Peter the Preacher she meditated upon God's providence in creating all things for our use.[192] During the Gospel she heard a voice, "I want to come to you." Then she asked, "Who are you?" He answered, "I am he who hung upon the cross. Do you want to go to heaven or remain here?" She answered, "I want whatever you want." He said, "Here are my mother and Catherine and Margaret and my twelve apostles and the twenty-four elders and martyrs and fifteen-thousand virgins and the nine choirs of angels, nine-thousand from each host. It was a year ago on Three Kings Day that I took you as my wife. Then I led you through the nine choirs of angels and when I came to Peter he complained that you had not prayed to him.[193] You should pray to him. And I asked

them all how pleasing you were to them. They answered that you were pleasing to them. Then I asked my mother. She also said, 'She pleases me well. I wish to do good to her.' Then I asked my heavenly Father, if you were pleasing to him. Then the heavenly Father said, 'She is pleasing to me. you cannot maintain her without me. I want to help you.' Then the Holy Spirit said, 'She cannot reach perfection without me. I want to bring her to perfection.'" Then Our Lord said, 'My Love, my Tender One, my Spouse, ask me for whatever you wish and I shall grant it to you. You should ask me because I come to you not only in order to make you holy, I come so that others may be made holy. None of those for whom you pray to me will remain separated from me and even if they are not immediately converted from their sins, even so I will remember them in their last days. None of your relatives will remain separated from me and forever there will be one among them in whom I will dwell. I will never separate myself from you and furthermore I wish to do more good for you than ever before. You should guard yourself against unnecessary speech because your words should be true and that comes from the fact that you will be given more of my grace than any other human being. I give you sixty-thousand souls from purgatory, who were thrown into misery and just as many sinners to be converted, who otherwise would never have been converted had it not seemed good to my providential wisdom to raise up another individual on earth through whom I would work such wonders. I give you the same number of good people to be confirmed in faith. Even before I created the world I intended this grace for you." And to our dear Lady he said, "My dear mother, let her be entrusted to you with the same faithfulness, as much as you love me." Then our Lady said, "I will gladly do that, my dear child. I will give her good things and be true to her." Our Lord turned to the angel Gabriel. "Approach me, Gabriel. You announced me to my mother and brought her good news from me. Now I entrust this one here to you so that you may lift up her prayers before my eyes." And the holy angel Gabriel did her much good. Our Lord raised his right hand and gave his divine blessing over her saying, "You shall be blessed forever." Then when this vision ceased her senses faded away. Then she saw many vipers and snakes around her and she was terribly afraid beyond all measure. Our Lord approached her in the form of a child. Then all the snakes and vipers vanished. Then Our Lord said, "I allow this to happen to you since no one has received such great grace so as not to be on guard at all times against the wiles of the devil. You should have no worries."

33. During the Mass on the feast of St. Peter the Preacher this sister began to ponder the works of love that Our Lord had accomplished on earth.[194] Then she was told, "I want to write my name on your heart so that it will never be erased. My name is 'Healer' and 'Savior.' I want to be deep within your heart and I will fill it up completely with myself and will lock it up with love and will always reside in it. I also want to write your name in my heart so that you will remain there forever. I will confess you in heaven before my mother and all saints and I will never deny you."[195]

34. Once on the feast of St. Dominic this sister was in suffering.[196] Then she thought, "Oh lord, St. Dominic! I always have such suffering on your feast. I will wither away in your Order." Then she was told, "Dominic has prayed for you today. I have commended you to him so that he will not send you so much suffering." She thought, "Oh Lord, indeed you give all things." Then she was told, "Why do you wonder about that? Since Dominic founded the Order, he became the intercessor for the Order and is so even today. He prays for every person when he commends them to me to do good for them."

35. Once on the summer solstice during Mass Our Lord came and said to her, "My Beloved, your mouth is sweeter than pure honey. Honey and milk are under your tongue.[197] My Darling, my Tender One, my Spouse and my Sister and my Child, these things concerning you were already in the thoughts of my providential wisdom even before I created the world. [When this monastery was founded I thought of three nuns in it who have been mine until

today and still continue to be mine. You are now the one who possesses my divine power and I proved that to be true in that I drew you forcefully out of the world and placed you in this monastery and as forcefully do good for you now as my most beloved and I shall never let up with my divine power until you have become a perfect human being. I also have another one here who belongs to my divine wisdom—this is Erlint. You should notice that she conducts herself wisely in all affairs of the Order. I have another here who belongs to my divine goodness— this is Christina Ebner].[198]

36. After that on the feast of St. Mary Magdalene, after Mass this sister was meditating upon Our Lord as Martyr and when she came to the point where he hung on the cross she asked Our Lord to come to her for the sake of Magdalene and another human being who is on earth.[199] Our Lord came and said, "For the sake of those for whom you have prayed I give you thirty-thousand souls from purgatory and as many sinners for conversion and the same number of devout people for strengthening in faith." Just then she heard the refectory bell. Then she said, "Oh no Lord, what should I do?" He said, "Go there under obedience. I shall go too." She went to table. When the reader began the reading, Our Lady, Mary Magdalene and Our Lord himself came and began with the lowest sister in the right choir and went up the row until he stood before this sister.[200] He said, "My Beloved," and sat down on her right side. Then she leaned down against his heart and lay against his breast until the sisters stood up[201]. Then she also stood up. She was led into her cell. There Our Lord granted her many good things beyond all measure and stayed with her and revealed many things to her. Then she felt herself to be far removed from other people.

37. Once this sister was betrayed by one of her friends. She thought, "Since everyone breaks faith with me Our Lord will also break faith with me." Then she cried from none until vespers. At vespers Our Lord came and asked, "My Beloved, my Tender One, my Betrothed, and my dear Spouse and my dear Child, what disturbs you? Why are you crying?" She said, "Oh dear Lord, since

everyone breaks faith with me, I fear that you also would break faith with me." Our Lord said, "Be assured, I will never break my divine faith with you. Since you have placed so much trust in me, before ever I let you be separated from me I would rather let heaven and earth pass away and create a new world. Whenever anything confuses or disturbs you, come to me and I will console you." Again she thought, "Oh no, Lord, now I have no one who does good to me, and I am dying." Then Our Lord said, "Now listen, before I leave you, I would rather (if it were appropriate) come myself and give you all the good things that any human being does for another."

38. After that on the feast of the Assumption of Our Lady this sister received Our Lord with the whole community.[202] When she had received Our Lord, he said to her, "My Beloved, you yourself should do good things for yourself, so that you can better serve me; and you should not be concerned about food and clothing, and should you wish to eat gold I would make even that serve to your benefit. I want to let all kinds of fruit of the earth grow for your sake, so that you will gain better nourishment with other people. For the sake of my friends I let fruit grow and should I let them grow for the sake of my enemies, there would be very little." She said, "Oh Lord, often your enemies have greater benefit from it than your friends." Our Lord said, "I do not want to give them hell both now and hereafter." She said, "Lord, dearest Lord, by all the love and by the trust I have in you, how dear am I to you?" Our Lord answered, "You are more beloved to me than any human being on earth, with the exception of one. And in a year from today you will be the most beloved on earth that I have. There are those on earth, who have served me better and will receive greater reward when they die. Yet my divine heart leans more to you than to any other human being." She said, "Oh Lord, how have I deserved this?" He said, "You have done this with nothing more than the great love that your heart has for me." And he forbade her to tell anyone except for one individual, whom he allowed her to tell. She asked him who that was, who was also so dear to him. He did not wish

to say anything about it then. He gave her thirty-thousand souls in purgatory and as many devout people to be strengthened and as many sinners to be converted. She asked, "Lord, I wonder why you always like to give by thirties?" Our Lord said, "I was betrayed for thirty pennies." She spent the whole day in grace and between the two Masses of Our Lady, Our Lord did good things for her.

39. Always on the feast of the Dedication of the Church, Our Lord gave great grace to her.[203] On one feast of the Dedication of the Church Our Lord gave her five-thousand souls and as many devout people and sinners. And to the sisters he gave five-thousand souls and as many good people and as many sinners. Our Lord gave to the people outside the monastery, who came to the church festival, five-thousand souls and as many devout people and sinners.

40. During the same time a high-ranking friar of the Order of Preachers arrived.[204] Then Our Lord commanded her to lay all her concerns before this same man. She did that. He considered and noted all her concerns and found that all was right and confirmed her in them. Then he commanded her to write it all down.[205]

41. On the octave of the same feast day the nuns received Our Lord and when this sister had received Our Lord he said to her, "You have received me spiritually no less than my mother conceived me bodily." And he said to her further, "Sit down, my Love, I will marry you." And he continued, "My Beloved, my Tender One, my Beautiful One, my love-sweet dear One, under your tongue is honey."[206] Then her soul said, "Lord, heaven is not enough for me, earth is too weak for me, for the consolation of angels, I care nothing, human consolation I do not want. Lord, if you have any love for me and give heed, then come yourself and do not send a messenger." And when she had said this, she was no longer able to speak nor to do anything else. She was outside herself. This continued until shortly before vespers when she came to herself again.

42. On the next day during the preaching Our Lord came to her and said, "I also wish to preach to you." He said to her, "Your mouth smells of roses and your body of violets. You are altogether

beautiful for nothing is lacking in you. For that reason you are beautiful since nothing is lacking in you.[207] You have captured me, just like a maiden who holds a young man captive in a lady's chamber and who knows well that if his friends were aware of it they would kill her and him. And then the maiden said to him, 'Who has forced you to come in here?' So he answers, 'Your beauty has drawn me, maiden. And what has moved you to permit me to enter?' Then she said, 'It is the great love that I bear for you.' See, thus divine love and love for you compels me at all times. You are so dear to me, even if I had suffered my martyrdom and death for no one other than for you alone, I would never regret what I have suffered. Now this maiden herself carried the key, and she let no one in or out, who could do wrong to her and compel the young man to flee. See, thus have you captured me in the lady's chamber of your heart. When you come, I am prepared. Your conscience holds the key. Now you should guard against letting anything else into your heart by which you will drive me out." Then her soul said, "Lord, heaven is nothing to me, earth is too weak for me, the consolation of angels I count as nothing and I do not want the consolation of humans. Lord, if you have any love for me and care for me, then come to me yourself and send no messenger and kiss me with the kiss of your mouth.[208] When she had said this, she sank down as before. After that when this sister had come to herself again Our Lord said to her, "As proof of this grace go to the Father Preacher and ask whether he had not preached about me and you." Then she asked the preacher what he had preached about. He said, "About Our Lord and you."

43. After that on the next day after Mass this sister had gone to someone and given that person a little golden ring. And immediately after that she went again to pray. Then Our Lord returned again with such great grace that all her senses were filled with this grace interiorly and exteriorly and he said, "My Beloved, my divine heart opens up to you with such great love, take whatever you wish. You can never ask me for so much that I will not be able to grant you

a thousand times more. How do you dare to go anywhere without my permission?" She said, "Lord, I am sorry." He said, "This has rightly happened to you. How do you dare to do anything without my permission?" She said, "Oh Lord, that person is also dear to you." Our Lord said, "What does it matter? I allow no one on earth for you except for myself." Then she thought, "That person must strengthen the grace that you have given me." Then Our Lord said, "Yes, should he confirm my grace for you? I confirm it for you myself. I am the most beautiful and most noble. I am the most loving and the richest. Everything in heaven and on earth serves me. Whatever you do not have I can give to you. There is nothing lacking in me." She said, "Lord, I see nothing lacking in you."[209] Then our dear Lord said, "My Beloved, lean down to my beloved heart and rest there like St. John." Then she bent down to his right side against his heart and it seemed to her that never in all her days was she so close to God as then and she was beside herself so that she had no control over herself.[210] Our Lord commanded the Father Preacher to give her Our Lord in the sacrament. He went on his way.

44. One day after that this sister lay there in grace from the Mass until vespers. For a time she was so weak that she could neither speak nor move, and again after a while she was so strong that she thought she could pull up a large tree from the earth. Now she asked Our Lord where this came from. Then Our Lord said, "Whenever I draw your soul out from your body into my divinity then you are sick, but whenever I pour my divinity into you, then you are strong."

45. Fourteen days later the Father Preacher returned and gave Our Lord to her and to four other sisters. As the youngest, she had to go alone. Then she thought to herself, "Oh Lord, I am now an imperfect human being, therefore I must go alone. Were I a good person, then I would not go alone." Then it was made known to her that she was not going alone at all because of the great love and desire she bore for Our Lord. She was not aware that anyone was going with her. When she had received Our Lord she asked,

"Lord, who came with me?" Then Our Lord said, "Peter and Paul." At the same time Our Lord gave her and also to the Father Preacher one-hundred-thousand souls from purgatory and as many devout people to be strengthened in faith and as many converted sinners. She became so unaware of herself that she also did not know what God was doing with her. When she came to herself again, she said, "Oh Lord, it seems indeed that I am the least worthy one, who has received you today because I do not know what good you have done for me." Our Lord raised his right hand and wrote her name on his heart and on his hands and feet and said, "See now, that I love you."[211]

46. On the same day the council gave her aunt an office.[212] Then that evening when the sister was sitting down at table, Our Lord came in the form of an eighteen-year old boy and led his mother by the hand. He said, "Do not be sad. Your aunt has been given an office." She said, "Oh no Lord! Who will do anything good to me? I have no one on earth but her." Then Our Lord said, "For that reason I will not abandon you. I will give you my mother so that she may care for you henceforth in all ways necessary to you. The words of the Lord's Prayer will be fulfilled in you, 'Hallowed be thy name.' My name will become holy in you so that you will never do anything unworthy either in word or in deed. The kingdom will come into your soul and be realized in all ways. There will be one will between you and me and those who are in heaven."

47. After that she said once more, that no one would enter the monastery without her knowing it beforehand from God. Also, no one in the monastery would die without her knowing it beforehand and after they had died it was made known to her how they should be helped. Sometimes she revealed this, but at other times she did not. She did not say because people would talk.

48. On the next day the sisters went to the altar. And when she received Our Lord, Our Lord spoke to her: "Today I want to give you my mother as your caregiver so that she may tend to you henceforth in all things necessary to you." The sister thought, "Oh no Lord, how shall I act towards her? She is too worthy for me."

Then Our Lord said, "Do you want Catherine or her?" She said, "Lord, since you do this out of your mercy, I want your mother." Then Our Lord said, "My dear mother, I entrust her to you and ask that you be good to her and be faithful to her. She should also be submissive to you." Our Lady said, "I shall now begin and show her that I will be faithful." She stood before God the Father and said, "Oh Lord, I remind you of the love that you showed me in giving me your only-begotten Son. For the sake of that same love I ask you to give me something for this person today." Then God the Father said, "I shall help you with my divine power so that she will resist strongly all vices." Then he raised three fingers and said, "I give you total certainty that she will never be separated from me." Our Lady stood before God the Son and said, "Lord, I remind you of my love as you lay forty weeks beneath my virginal heart, so that you will give me something for this person out of your mercy." He said, "I will do that. I will help her with my divine wisdom so that she may accomplish all good things wisely according to my all-loving will and I will give her great reward for meditating upon and contemplating my martyrdom every day as if she were standing by me at the cross in reverent prayer." Our Lady went before the Holy Spirit and said, "Lord, you who bring about all good things, and have also made me perfect in all things, give me something out of your goodness for this person today." Then the Holy Spirit said, "I will never cease from granting her my goodness until she becomes the most perfect of all human beings." Then Our Lady went before St. John the Evangelist and said, "Dear John, give me something today for this sister since she loves you so much." Then he said, "I will gladly do it. I will help you to care for her." Then Our Lady said, "I myself care well for her. Give her something else." He promised her that he would pray to Our Lord for her. Our Lady asked St. John the Baptist also to give her something. He promised her that he would pray to the Lord for her. Our Lady also asked St. Dominic and St. Peter the Apostle to give her something. Then St. Peter said, "Dear Lady, tell her she may pray as much to me as she prays to St. John the Evangelist." They promised her that they would also pray to Our Lord for her. Our Lady asked all the angels and all the saints to give her something so that she would enjoy it and thank the Holy Trinity for them every day. Then they all said together, "We will never cease praying for her to the Holy Trinity until she becomes a perfect human being." This sister thought in her heart, "Oh Lord, what a great grace this grace is. Had someone saddened me more than a thousand times you would have made me forget it." Our Lord forbade her from taking revenge for anything and ordered her to recite the *Te Deum* three times, while making the venia three times.[213] Our Lord gave her thirty-thousand souls from purgatory and as many devout people to be strengthened and as many sinners to be converted.

49. On the feast of the eleven-thousand virgins a widow was received into the monastery.[214] She prayed for her. Our Lord said, "She will not remain here without your prayers. She will become a good person and remain here." And the eleven-thousand virgins came to their feast. Our Lord said, he would grant to the nun everything for which she asked him on her knees. Then the bell rang to go to table and it was the week when this sister had to serve. She said, "Oh no, dear Lord, how shall I serve since I am so sick?" Then Our Lord said, "Go, I will help you to serve." She went and served at table and he helped her to serve diligently.

50. After that, Advent began and Our Lady took this sister under her care and gave her special grace every day and Our Lord himself did so as well. And then during the midnight Mass at Christmas when the priest intoned the *Gloria in excelsis*, Our Lady came carrying the naked child in her arms and went from one sister to the other and she looked especially at some and showed them her Child and gave her little Child into the arms of two sisters and whenever the name of Our Lord was sung in the *Gloria in excelsis*, Our Lady made a profound bow. Then Our Lady came to the sister—she had two friends—and it seemed to this sister that Our Lady was not well disposed to the two sisters who were her

special friends and she said, "Dear Lady from heaven, I ask you not to deprive my friends because of me. Be good to them." Then Our Lady said she would gladly do that. Our Lady placed herself in front of the sister and it seemed to this sister that her own heart opened up and Our Lady took her little Child and placed him in her heart. Then her heart closed up again and Our Lady made the sign of the cross over her heart saying, "You will remain in this heart forever." Then Our Lord did good things for her beyond all measure. Our Lord said, "Hear how my beloved people, whom I have chosen from all the world, sing." And he said, "I will give them something for your sake so that they will not begin to say that I do nothing for the sake of my friend." Then he said, "I will give them three gifts for your sake. The first—that this monastery will never burn down; the second—that you will never be separated; and third—that no one from this community will be separated from me. This will be accomplished with great wonders." During the next Mass Our Lord came as an eight-year-old child. No one noticed him. At the third Mass he came as a mighty king and was beautiful beyond all measure. This sister was confused because he disappeared so quickly. This sister thought, ["Oh dear, was this appearance true or has the Evil One deceived me?" She was very distressed. Then when she received Our Lord, Our Lord said, "Why do you not believe? Do you think that the Evil Spirit is able to open your heart or that I would allow him to deceive you or any person on such a festive day and during the holy Mass?]215 ("Oh dear Lord, such a thing I have not deserved from you and I am unworthy, since regrettably I have never lived a day as I ought according to your praise," and she was in great distress and in great fear of Our Lord. Then when she received Our Lord with the whole community after the third Mass, Our Lord made it known to her that he gives her these things out of love and not because she has earned them and said,) "Woe! How little you believe and how much it takes to make you believe. When I appeared today during Mass as a child and the nuns honored me—that meant that much honor was offered me during my childhood. At the other Mass when I came as an eight-year-old boy and they paid no attention to me —that means that no one paid attention to me for my first eight years on earth and no one honored me. At the third Mass, when you saw me as I had come of age—that means that when I was on earth and came to my day—they killed me." Our Lord gave her thirty-thousand souls from purgatory and as many devout people confirmed in faith and as many sinners converted and promised to give her the same number on St. John the Evangelist Day and said, "I will not be changed into you, rather you should be changed into me."[216] Then the sister was in such grace that she did not know what good God did for her and further she sat there like a corpse.

51. Afterward on St. Stephen Day during the Mass Our Lord came to this sister and said, "These graces I had already intended for you before I created the world.[217] And when I poured your soul into your body—it was on Three Kings Day—your soul peered into my divinity and I said to your soul, "My Beloved! Because of this you must have ever more of me than others and if you did not have me, you would not be able to live.[218] So she was in grace the whole day until compline. After compline, Our Lord came and then God the Father said, "I will give you my only-begotten Son. What then will you give me?" Then the sister said, "Lord, my soul and my body." Then the Lord said, "They are already mine." She said, "Oh Lord, what should I give you then?" Our Lord said, "You should give me everyone whom you have ever met so that you will set your heart on no one but on me alone." She said, "Lord, I will gladly do that." Then the Father said, "Then I give you my only-begotten Son." Then God's Son said, "I give you the Holy Spirit." Then the Holy Spirit said, "I give you all the virtues and I will confirm them in you." It seemed to her that her soul was reading the *Te Deum laudamus*.[219] She was so out of her senses that she could not speak any more. Then she said, "Lord, how should I thank you for these great graces?" Then Our Lord said, "Speak to my dear mother so that she will thank me for you." Then this sister said, "My dear Lady,

thank your only Son." Then Our Lady stood up and knelt down before Our Lord and said, "My dear child, now let it be an offering of thanks to you that I carried you forty weeks beneath my heart and that I brought you into the world and I brought you up lovingly and tenderly, and led you away into Egypt and that I never left you in any need and that I followed after you to the cross and suffered along with you at your martyrdom and that afterward I still lived a few years on earth. My much beloved Child, let these be thanks to you instead for this person." Then Our Lord said, "You have thanked me well." Our Lord said to the sister, "My Dear, why do you love me?" Then she said, "Lord, because you are faithful and because you are beautiful and because you are rich and because you are gentle and because you can fulfill all hearts and because you are merciful."

52. On the Sunday before Shrove Tuesday, this sister thought about the mission that Our Lord had with his twelve apostles. Then Our Lord came with his twelve apostles and said to this sister, "Look, now I have come with my apostles and also your betrothed— St. John the Evangelist!" Then she said, "Oh Lord, why have you given him to me as my betrothed? You are doing this to me out of hostility because you do not want me yourself." Then Our Lord said, "I recognize well that you love him, therefore I too speak so lovingly about him to you." She said, "Lord, I want to invite you." As soon as she had said this she regretted it. Then Our Lord said, "I will come, there is no need for regret." He named the day—the Annunciation to Our Lady in Lent. Then she said, "Lord, I cannot wait so long. It is too long a time until then." Then Our Lord said, "Then take White Sunday or a week later."[220] She said, "Lord, I invite you and your mother and Saint John the Evangelist with all twelve apostles and St. John the Baptist with all patriarchs and prophets, and my lord, Saint Dominic with all confessors and all saints and all angels and King David with his harp." The sister thought, "Oh Lord, how should I show you honor?" Then Our Lord said, "You should recite the antiphon *Te Deum Patrem ingenitum* to my divine

power one-thousand times and one-thousand *Pater Nosters* to my divine wisdom and the *Veni Sancte Spiritus* to my divine goodness one thousand times and to my Holy Body the *Beati immaculati* thirty times and one thousand *Aves* to my mother and to the angels ten *Te Deums* and to all saints one thousand times the *Gloria Patri* and to all believers one thousand times the *Requiem aeternam*.[221] You should take the discipline three times reciting three *Misereres* each time using a hackle until you bleed and you should cry sweet tears." The sister did all this as the Lord had commanded her.

53. Then on the vigil of the Chair of St. Peter Our Lord came to the sister during Mass and so did Our Lady and St. Peter the Apostle.[222] Then Our Lord said to St. Peter, "Peter, I command you, when she comes, to open heaven to her at prime or at whatever time she comes." Then St. Peter said, "Lord, I will gladly do that." St. Peter said to the sister, "Make your confession and I will give you absolution." Then the sister answered, "Oh dear lord St. Peter, hear my confession tomorrow, but give me absolution now." He gave her absolution and gave her Our Lord's Body and gave her the blessing "*Benedictio Dei*."[223] Then the sister said to Our Lady, "My much beloved Lady, of what does your Son accuse me?" Then Our Lady answered, "Dearly Beloved, with what does he charge me? Indeed, he never left me in any need." Then the sister said, "Oh Lady from heaven, you may not speak so of yourself, since I am indeed a great sinner." Then our Lady said, "It does me no harm to take on humility to myself."

54. On the next day the sister was sitting before a crucifix. St. Peter the Apostle came and she confessed to him and he gave her absolution and for a penance a *Miserere* and showed her the keys of the kingdom which were silver, and behind on the ring he carried a cross and Peter said, "Come at whatever time you wish—at prime, terce, sext or none, and I will let you in."

55. After that on the next Sunday which was St. Matthias Day, the sister thought to herself, that Our Lord had given her promises on that day and she cried bitterly for Our Lord.[224] And nonetheless

her soul rejoiced in her body. The crying and praying were taken from her then. Then God the Father said, "Be at peace, I will free you from the prison of your body and take you up into my divine grace and will lead you into the kingdom, that I prepared for you from the beginning of the world." Then God the Son said, "So I will give you myself, because I can show you no more love with anything other than myself. Here I give you my humanity to enjoy and there in eternity my divinity and humanity. I myself will come to your death and will take your soul into my arms, that I stretched out to you on the Holy Cross. And I will lead you through the nine choirs of angels and will place you among my most loved ones and will crown you with all the good that I have ever done. Inasmuch as I have given you more good here than to others I will give you even more as a reward in eternal life. Then you will be crowned with the purity of your heart." He said, "I will press your soul to my divinity so that you will be as like me as is possible." Our Lord stretched out his arms and pressed her soul deeply into his divine heart. With this it was so well with her that she thought it could never be better for her. He said to her, "I will be yours forever and will belong to all those for whom you pray to me—I will even be in purgatory or wherever you bid me go." And he said, "You should be gentle." She was also fed on the Body of Our Lord and all the things that have happened to her at other times when she received Our Lord also happened to her on this day. Our Lord said, "I also want to grant grace to the monastery. I will forgive them all their sins and will give you even more grace. I will give thirty-thousand souls from purgatory and as many devout people to confirm in faith and as many sinners for conversion." Then the Holy Spirit said, "I will make you so perfect with my divine goodness that nothing will be lacking in you." Then Our Lady said, "I will pray to the Holy Trinity for you every day until he has brought you to what he promised you and I will be with you always and will be kinder to you than if you had been a maidservant." Then St. Peter said to the other apostles, "I am the oldest. I am indeed your representative."

And he said to the sister, "We will pray to Our Lord for you every day until he fulfills in you what he has promised you." St. John the Baptist said to the patriarchs and the prophets, "I will speak." And then he said to the sister, "We all will pray for you to Our Lord until he brings you to what he has promised you." Then the sister said to King David, "Dear King David, what will you give me?" He said, "I will play the harp for you until your soul departs from you as I have already done for many others until their souls left them." Then all the saints said they would pray to God for her to lead her to what he had promised her. Then all the angels said, "We will now begin to praise Our Lord because he has been so good to you." And they began to sing *Gloria in excelsis* according to the manner sung during the octave and also the *Te Deum laudamus*.

56. One time on the vigil of St. John the Evangelist, this sister desired Our Lord.[225] Then Our Lord came. Although she was not yet well prepared for it he gave her much love and grace. Then she desired him to come at another time because she wished to serve St. John. Our Lord did that and came at another time and said, "On Holy Thursday night, as I washed the feet of my apostles, when I came to St. Peter it was only necessary for me to wash his feet. So I say to you, "My Love, it is necessary for me to wash you all over. First, your eyes so that they will look at me alone and also your ears so that they will hear my teaching and the teachings of my teachers so that you will keep them; and your nose so that it will detect the falsehood of the world and know that faithfulness is found in no one, but me alone. Your heart should belong to me alone and have no one except me. Your tongue should speak the truth for it should rightly be that those who do not speak the truth should have their tongues ripped out. Your mouth should praise me at all times. Your hands should do my works, Your feet should walk in my ways. You should gladly come to me. All the strength of all your limbs should be consumed in my service. I have purchased heaven for you by my death. You must serve me, I have acted like a man, who offers his life for the good of another and says to him,

'I will give you the good or my life.' I have given my life for your sake and am dead for you and you must give your strength for the sake of the kingdom of heaven. To those who serve me I will give the heavenly kingdom. If the whole world served me I would give it to the whole world."

57. On St. John's Day this sister desired Our Lord with her whole heart and said, "On no Beloved, now I have no one but you and you do not want to come to me!"[226] She cried and complained miserably. Then Our Lord came and asked, "Why are you crying?" Then she replied, "For you, Lord." Then Our Lord said, "I am here as true God just as I rose from the dead on Easter morning." He spoke many more words of comfort which she could not take note of out of pure joy.

58. On the feast of the Annunciation this sister received Our Lord's Body.[227] When she received Our Lord she was so taken out of herself that she had no awareness of herself and this continued until midday. After that she came to herself again. Then she was so filled with God in all her limbs that she thought if she had more of him she would die. Then Our Lord said, "I want to tell you that I have pulled out your soul from all your members and from all your powers and I have drawn and pulled your soul into the wild Godhead and into the wilderness of my divinity.[228] I have fed you with my eternal fruit." Then she asked, "Lord, what is your eternal fruit?" Then he answered, "That is my only-begotten, eternal Son and he has poured out and filled you with his eternal love so that you will recognize the truth." From that same day until Easter she was so full of love that at all times she thought her soul would overflow from love. On Easter Day when she received Our Lord, Our Lord said, "Go back into your humanity, you cannot always remain in my divinity." And Our Lord showed her a carbuncle and held it up in the sunlight and said, "See, the carbuncle does not shine nearly so beautifully as in the sunlight and if there be any kind of flaw in it, one sees it best in the sunlight. See here, it is the same with you and with all my beloved friends—on them I shine with

the brilliant radiance of my divinity and there is indeed little that can be seen in them. You flash and sparkle like a carbuncle in the sunlight." And he showed her a garden in which grew all sorts of plants, fruit and especially flowers that opened up toward the sun. "See the blossom that has opened toward the sun, in it the sun shines. Perhaps there can be a little worm sitting on the little blossom so that the ray of sunlight cannot reach the inner part, just as small sins hinder my friends so that they often must go without my grace.

59. After that she was in such grace from Easter to Pentecost and in such divine love that whether she ate or drank or whether awake or asleep, whether alone or with other people, unceasingly it seemed to her as if her soul would go out of itself because of true divine love. On Pentecost she came to herself and when she became aware of herself and her members, she lay there as if dead and all the nuns in the monastery believed that she would die. She was sick the whole year through and was never healthy on any day. For two years she lay in such suffering from the illness during which no day ended without her wishing that she would die in order to be free of it. Without divine consolation she bore this for two years because as often as Our Lord the Beloved God did good to her, she was so out of herself that she knew nothing more about herself. After that this suffering lasted three more years, but once in a while she received consolation from God in that he did not wish to leave her in suffering. Often this was so great that she cried and thought to herself, "Lord Jesus Christ, what will happen to me? I would rather suffer death than this illness." So it continued for five years and she lay in immeasurable suffering. One day during Mass in Lent before a crucifix, this was taken away from her with such great grace about which she could not speak up to her death. One day she had lain down and slept. Then a voice said to her, "Whoever has any illness, should stand before a crucifix and read the psalm *Deus, Deus meus respice* and the antiphon *Christus factus obediens est pro nobis obediens usque ad mortem, mortem autem crucis*.[229] She should recite these seven times with seven venias—five to the

five holy wounds of Our Lord and one to his head and another to all his members and should say:

> With suffering I am surrounded,
> A cross in me is founded,
> in my suffering need.
> From this free me Lord Jesus Christ,
> by your bitter death.[230]

Say that every day and you will be free from suffering." When she had recited this prayer several days, she was delivered from her suffering.

60. In a village there was a builder named Herman Kramer. He had been sick for ten long years so that he wanted to commit suicide and had already sought the opportunity to do so twice and wanted to accomplish it, but people came and prevented him. Then he came to the monastery and sent for this sister and complained to her about his suffering with much moaning and crying and asked her to pray to God for him to help him out of his suffering. She told him to recite five *Pater Nosters* and five *Ave Marias* to the five wounds of Our Lord and one *Pater Noster* to Our Lord's head and one to all his members. Then the man said, "Sister, my suffering is often so great that I am not even able to pray." She said, "Then say only "Jesus Christ" and call upon the Holy Name." Then the man said, "My suffering is often so great that I cannot speak." She said, "Then think about the Name of our beloved Lord Jesus Christ and hold it in your heart." Then the man said, "Dear Sister I will gladly do everything that you tell me and have told me and I ask Our Lord to help me out of my suffering. I know well that he appears in your presence and would like you to ask him about this." She had never seen him before and had never heard anything about him. Then she asked God with great earnestness to take away his sufferings. Shortly thereafter he returned and thanked God for her saying, "May God be thanked, praised and honored forever! He has shown

his mercy to me and has heard your prayer for me. I am saved from my suffering. I will pray to God for you until my death even more than for my mother." From then on he came to the monastery every year and thanked her especially. And she commanded him to say nothing about it to anyone.[231] However, he told his wife and children and became a thoroughly good man.

61. There was a man at Nuremberg called Marquard Tockler. He came to the monastery to visit this sister and asked her to implore God for him and asked her what sort of life he should lead in order to gain God's favor. He told her he was greatly tempted. She had never seen him before and had never heard of him. She told him to enter the Order of St. Augustine and from now on to follow God and her. He entered the Order and when the first year in the Order had come to an end he visited her in the monastery. She asked him whether he had lost his temptation. He said, "No, I have not lost it. It comes now more frequently than before." She asked him what the temptation was. He said, "I have had it for nine years and have never confessed it nor said anything to anyone. I do not think it would do any good to tell you." Immediately Our Lord revealed to her his grace and mercy in that she recognized all his suffering and said, "Woe to you, poor man, do you want to let your body and soul be overcome by the devil?" She said, "You are sorely tempted, I know for certain you want to kill yourself." Immediately he told her that is true and he wept bitterly and asked her to pray for him to Our Lord saying. "If I should continue in this suffering I will lose my senses or do the act." Then she taught him this prayer that was already written before and asked Our Lord earnestly to take away his sufferings. He traveled then to Paris where he had been sent. After several years he returned and told her that he had lost his suffering and would pray to Our Lord for her until his death. He became a rather good master of Holy Scripture.

62. One day Our Lord did something kind for her. He said to her, "I will lead my Love into the garden of love and will show her the fruit of love and will make her a wreath of white lilies from my

divine and human purity and will crown my love and set upon her head a crown of diverse fruits. This means that I will give you a share in the love of the patriarchs, the confessors and the virgins." She also saw flowers that were not yet completely open. Then Our Lord Jesus Christ said to her, "See, my Love, this means that no one in this world can grasp eternal life. This was given to you here only to recognize, but there you will see me forever. Beloved, what would you have me do with you? Your heart is mine, I want to be in your heart. I have chosen your heart for me and had I chosen for me all human hearts I would be as good to them as to you. What is it to you that I am doing something with your heart? I will remain in your heart forever. My heart is yours, I will give it to you. You should ask me for whatever you want. Your soul is mine, your body is mine. Therefore you should not be concerned about whatever I do with you. Unwillingly would I do anything that was not good for you, as you have already seen. I am better able to observe you than you can observe yourself. Whenever something bothers you, come before the cross and complain to me about what bothers you. I will remove it."

63. On the Assumption of Our Lady she received Our Lord.[232] Then our Lord Jesus Christ was very good to her. He spoke lovingly to her, "My Beloved, sweet as sugar or honey, my Tender One, my Pure One, you are mine and I am yours. We are united and shall remain united forever. My Child, you should drink from my hands and my feet and from my side, from the fount of love from which flowed blood and water when I died on the cross." Then she experienced special grace beyond all measure and all external works or things were taken from her.

64. She had a companion who was a holy nun named Sister Christina of Kornburg.[233] She was very dear to her. She told her all the good that Our Lord had done for her during her lifetime. One day she said to her, "Dear Christina, tell me something about the good things Our Lord has done for you." Then she answered, "I will tell you nothing about it." No matter how much she asked,

she would tell her nothing. She became very sad and asked Our Lord to reveal to her the confidences that he had with this sister. Three days before Christmas while she was sitting in her cell, an angel came in despite the locked door.[234] He was so brilliant and beautiful that the cell was completely illumined more beautifully than with sunshine. Then her heart was so full of grace and sweetness that she thought it was Our Lord and would have liked to call to him as if it were God himself. Then the angel said, "I am not God. Our Lord Jesus Christ sent me here to you to reveal all the hidden secrets that he shares with your companion Christina of Kornburg." And he told her all about the good God had done for her ever since her childhood and when he had finished telling her she saw him no more. On the third day after Christmas she went to her companion and asked her yet again to tell her what good God had done for her. Still she did not want to tell her anything. Then she said, "Since you will tell me nothing I will tell you." She began and told her everything that she knew just as the angel had told it to her. When she had finished speaking, the other one said, "Truly you know it as well as I even though I have told no one. With the same faith in which you asked me, I now ask you, who told you about this? Until now there has been no one who knew. How do you know this then?" She told her how the angel had revealed it to her as written above. Then she was filled with awe and broke out into tears and said, "These are the wonders of God that he does not hide from his friends. How precisely he has told you all that he has done with me for these seventy yours! Since he himself does not conceal this from you so I too will conceal nothing about him and from now on I will tell you everything up to my death." This same Christina was a true mirror of all holiness in our monastery up to her death.[235]

65. Test and note well what wonders God does for his friends in heaven and on earth. Even to those who have not been dedicated to him from childhood he gives his love nonetheless. In spirit she saw a tree that was so beautiful that she could not comprehend it and did

not know how to describe it. The tree was so well formed in height and breadth that one could wish for nothing more beautiful. All the branches on the tree were made of pure gold. On the branches a red-hot fire burned next to the gold, but did the tree no harm. The leaves were as green as could be. The fruit was early ripe colored both green and red and where the branches parted so that one could see through the tree this sequence was written in golden letters:

> *Rex Salomon fecit templum*
> *cuius instar et exemplum*
> *Cristus et ecclesia.*
> King Solomon made the Temple
> which is an image and example
> of Christ and the Church.

Our Lord Jesus Christ was sitting half in and half out of the tree. The tree enfolded him as if he had grown out of it. He wore the most joyous attire with heavenly decoration that she knew not how to describe. He extended his arms a little and was full of joy. His joy she could not compare with anything except himself when he wished to lead a soul to heaven. His face shone like the sun. When she saw her most beloved Lord Jesus Christ she could neither speak nor make a gesture and she was satisfied merely to look at him the whole time in such joy. Our Lord Jesus Christ spoke to her with such sweet words saying, "My Beloved." These words were said so softly and sweetly that she could never forget them. When she came to herself again this vision was interpreted for her by Our Lord Jesus Christ who said to her, "The tree that you saw is the Father in heaven and that you saw me in the tree means that I am in the Father and he is in me. The fire that you saw that encircled all the branches of the tree means that the Holy Spirit is in both of us. However that may be: no mind on earth can grasp or ponder that. Yet in eternal joy there you, my chosen one, will understand it. Still here below you should believe it in simplicity and do not think about it too much." This was also explained to her: when she saw the above mentioned sequence written in golden letters where the branches divide— that means that all who belong in eternal life are inscribed in the Holy Trinity never to be erased. The ripe fruit that hung on the tree means the love that he conveys to his most beloved one, to whom he reveals the secrets of his divinity as well as his humanity. The fruit was red and green—this means that he gives them suffering and sweetness. Because to whomever he grants his goodness he allows suffering as well. Our Lord said, "I am ready for all sinners who turn to me." Then she said, "Oh loving Lord, Oh most beloved Lord, convert us poor sinners to yourself. Remember that you became man for our sake."

66. One time she was exetatrix, but when she had to get up for matins she was so sick that she could not do it.[236] Then Our Lord said to her, "Get up! I will help you." Immediately she got up and her heart was full of divine love and as she made her rounds he went along with her through the dormitory to all the cells and from him streamed such light and radiance that she did not know what she was doing. In the morning a nun named Sister Elsbet Ortlieb, the subprioress, came to her and said, "Tell me, who was helping you to make the rounds last night?"[237] She did not want to tell. Then she said, "Even if you do not say, I saw that Our Lord Jesus Christ was with you and such light came from him and such pure radiance and it was so bright that one could see in my cell better from his brilliance than from the sun shining brilliantly on the clearest of days."

67. One day the nanny who raised her came to the monastery. Then the nuns went to her and asked her about the child and said, "Tell us, dear Kunigunde, have you ever experienced anything special about her?" Then she answered, "Yes, one day as I was sitting by the cradle leaning on it I fell asleep. Then the most beautiful lady that my eyes have ever seen came and she was wearing a blue mantle. This mantle was so wide that if it had ever been unfolded it would have covered the whole world. She asked me, "Kunigunde,

are you sleeping?" and woke me up. Then I said, "Not I, Madam." So she asked me three times whether I was sleeping and each time I answered, "Not I, Madam!" Then she said, "May this child be entrusted to you and know that she will become a good person and many sinners will be converted through her." Then I asked, "Lady, who are you?" She said, "I am the Mother of Mercy." And as soon as she had said that I never saw her again. Indeed my heart was so filled with grace that I became happier taking better care of the child than before. Once at night a light shone above the cradle. It was more brilliant than sunshine and was so bright that I could not bear it. Then I picked up the cradle with the child in it and ran out of the room. Everyone in the house said to me, "Kunigunde, what are you doing? What is it with you?" I answered, "A light came from heaven and wanted to take my child from me and the light was so bright that I was blinded by it."

68. On St. Alexius Day God revealed to her that all people who traveled to the shrine of Our Lady in Aachen and who sought her grace and the grace of her Child in true Christian faith and with the right intention—none of these would ever be separated from God.[238] And even those who do not go there on pilgrimage, but only go there in prayer with the right intention, who would otherwise go if they could manage it, especially people in a religious state who can not travel—all these will have great reward and even greater since they cannot see the sanctuary and nonetheless turn their senses and desire to it especially when they would have gladly borne the burdens and hardships that pilgrims must endure, but can only make the journey in devout prayer. The sister then wanted to know how much a pilgrim who set out for Aachen should pray daily. She was told by God: a pilgrim should leave out nothing of the usual prayers and in addition should recite daily one thousand *Ave Marias*. During the pilgrimage they should abstain from meat both going and coming back. They should make a good confession, receive Our Lord's Body and guard themselves against discord. Our Lord said, "Religious people, note this well, lose their reward

through disharmony. Even when they have served me diligently, yet show wrath and impatience, do they imagine they will have great reward? They lose their reward because it has made them sour."

69. One day she related that ever since she entered the monastery she had beaten herself with a juniper switch so often and so long that the switch was ruined.[239] Since she no longer had the juniper switch she took up a thistle rod whose seeds were as sharp as needles. She used that throughout the whole year until the thistles were ruined. After that she grabbed a hackle and beat herself severely until blood flowed out from her and used that so long that she became sick and remained so for a whole year. When she recovered she acquired a hedgehog pelt. For a while she beat herself with that until she could no longer bear it. She said that she had lived twenty years in the monastery during which no day passed without her own suffering or that of her friends. She wore a hair-shirt so long and became so weak that she had to take it off. After she had taken off the hair-shirt she had the pain for many years. In her younger days she wrapped a cord made of hairs and an iron chain around her. While she was still in the world after a bed had been prepared for her to lie down she placed a board on the bed beneath her sheet and lay upon it. When she got up in the morning she removed the board and hid it so that no one would see it.

70. In the year of Our Lord 1336 a knight called Eberhard Schutz was living in the castle of Hohenstein.[240] He had a wife, but was so bad that one had to wonder how a human being could live with so much sinfulness. He was a servant of this world and had completely forgotten our Lord Jesus Christ in his heart, except that he still had Christian faith and was drawn to good people whenever he heard about them. He went to a hermit named Simon and asked him to pray to God for him so that he would turn away from sinning. Then the hermit said to him, "You should go to the monastery of Engelthal in which by God's mercy lives a nun (whom he named). The prayer of this nun should convert you from your sins. Our Lord shows her such love that he denies her nothing." The knight traveled

to the monastery and sent for her. When she was called she did not know who it was because she had never seen him before. Then she said, "I do not want to go. I do not know who he is." He rode to the monastery a second time and sent for her urgently asking why she could not come to him. He came a third time and sent for the prioress and asked her earnestly to help him see the sister. He did not want to leave until he had seen her. The prioress and other sisters begged her earnestly to go to him. Then she went for the praise of God. She received him and asked what he wanted from her and why he had sent for her. He said, "The hermit called Simon told me about you." Then she said, "I do not know who he is." She asked him whether he liked to pray and recite the canonical hours. He said, "What do you mean by 'hours?' I pray scarcely five or three or even one Our Father in a day." She asked, "Do you not fast?" He said, "No, to me Friday is like any other day." He said, "I am already forty years old and have never yet received God's Body. And now I ask you, for the sake of God, to pray for me to God so that he may convert me from all my sins, and teach me how I should pray now and what I should do to gain God's favor." Then she said, "You should guard your eyes against all unnecessary sights and whatever you see that is contrary to God you should always turn to the good in your heart. You should guard yourself against all unnecessary and loose words. Whenever you hear such speech you should never say a word, but if you can not avoid it and have to speak, then you should at all times speak so that such evil talk will diminish and not be spread about. And you should guard yourself against going to any unnecessary place. Wherever you know people who live contrary to God you should never go there, but if you must go guard yourself against sin and carry our Lord Jesus Christ in your heart and trust completely in him to turn you away from your sins and help you to become a good man." She taught him to recite five Our Fathers, one for each of the five wounds of Our Lord and to add to each Our Father a special petition and said to him, "Whenever you are no longer able to pray then entrust yourself to the five wounds of Our Lord." She taught him to say the *Ave Maria* to Our Lady and to add a special petition to it. She said to him, "With that entrust yourself to Our Lady also whenever you can not pray much and then say that." Then he cried intensely and said, "I have a wife who is sick and dying. I will do what you tell me." Four weeks later she died. Then he returned and told her that his wife had died and asked her how he should live from now on. She said, "You should take the Queen of Heaven, the Mother of God, as your wife and should earnestly pray to her and fast in her honor every Saturday. If you are satisfied with the heavenly Virgin, I would like that. If, however, you can not avoid taking another you should first tell me her name. I know well who she is, who will become yours. The one who is to be yours should remain in total purity with you." She meant Our Lady Mary, but he thought she meant a worldly wife or a virgin and that pleased him very much. If she had immediately told him about deep prayer he would not have been able to believe it. She asked him whether he had not improved. Then he said, "Yes, when I was with you and spoke with you, God gave me true contrition for all my sins. I can cry for my sins and am able to confess and to fast and to keep vigil and to pray and am able to do all things that belong to God." Then he asked her how he should pray for the soul of his wife. She told him to recite thirty-thousand *Ave Marias*. He could not recite all of them in four weeks. He told her that afterward when he returned to the monastery. She wondered about that in her heart. After that she was in divine grace. Our Lord Jesus Christ said to her, "I will give you the knight of Hohenstein, Eberhard, so that he will be converted from all his sins. You should tell him to go to the monastery of Kaisheim and become a monk. I will confirm the marriage of my mother with him. No other will do for him. You should tell him that when he comes again." Then she thought, "Oh Lord, what shall I say to him? Probably he will never do it." She became sad and never in her days was she in such distress. After that on the vigil of the Circumcision of Our Lord he came back and told her about a young woman.[241] She was very pretty and wanted to be good to him. All his friends had advised him to marry her and now the decision is laid on no one but God and her to tell him whether she is the right one. Then she said, "No, she is not for you." She told him what Our Lord had commanded. When he realized that he should become a monk he seemed quite sad and fell silent, saying nothing for so long that one could have recited fifty *Ave Marias*. Then he said, "Sister, ask God to give me his divine grace. Otherwise it can not happen." Immediately he left. Then she went to pray in the choir and asked God fervently to have mercy on the man and to make of him a man who lived according to His dearest will. Then Our Lord Jesus Christ said to her, "With this man I will let you know how much I really love you." Then someone wanted to lock the choir. She went out and her heart cried out to Our Lord through the whole night to have mercy on him. In the morning after Mass she asked him how he was doing. He said, "When I left you yesterday I was so depressed that I had to lie down immediately, but I remained awake and could not fall asleep. As I lay there I heard such a rumbling noise as when a bad storm approaches in summer. I jumped up and thought, Our Lady will certainly come to comfort me. Then I saw a blue fog that enshrouded me and filled my room. Then a ray shot down from heaven into the crown of my head and struck deeply into my heart and was so hot and fiery from divine love that I thought I was burning alive and I threw off the blanket. When the ray came into my heart it spread out into all my limbs. When I perceived the heat in all my limbs I began to laugh and to cry so that all the servants who lay near to me in the room got up and asked what was wrong with me. I could say nothing to them. The laughing and crying grew ever louder so that everyone spending the night in the guest house got out of bed. All of them watched with me through the night. I forgot all worldly things completely and never can I return to the world. From that moment on I wanted nothing more than to become a monk. Beg the Lord for the monks of Kaisheim to accept me." Divine grace grew and increased in him. When he sat at table among many people or in church among the public he broke out laughing and crying so that all the people were amazed and said, "If the man in distress has been drawn into jubilation we should not leave him." After that on Corpus Christi he went to the monastery and received the Body of Our Lord, which he had never before received.[242] He received it with such devotion that everyone who saw it was moved. And God granted him such great grace that everyone who heard about it wondered and praised God for it. After that he was admitted into the monastery of Kaisheim into the gray Order.[243] With great joy he brought the news to Engelthal that he had been admitted and said, "Pray to Our Lord that he confirm his grace in me when I enter the monastery. And if God gives me his grace then I will pray to God for you more than for all others who are on earth." After that on the Assumption of Mary he put on the habit.[244] She asked the Lord to strengthen him in a good way of life and she prayed with true zeal when she was in great suffering because she had compassion for him and thought, "Oh Lord, if he should run away from the Order all those who speak against me throughout the land will win." The next Christmas she asked Our Lord again to strengthen him in a good life. So that God's honor would be accomplished in him she would give up all the good Our Lord had done for her spiritually. During the same Christmas season after the Feast of the Three Kings it happened as he stood in the choir of his monastery [that a beautiful woman dressed in heavenly attire appeared to him and brought him three small rolls scarcely the size of three nutmegs and told him to eat them.[245] And when he ate them it seemed to him as if the sweetest drink had been given to him in his mouth that had ever been sent from heaven and this spread throughout his limbs so that they were filled up with divine sweetness and divine grace. This grace lasted in him more than twelve years, and when he came to pray he was filled up and overcome by divine grace. Often among the people he was so filled with divine grace that he had to go away from them.] (and how he and all the other novices wanted to approach the altar to receive the Body of Our Lord. And then the first novice went up, but the previously mentioned Eberhard was the youngest in religion and therefore he had to go last. And as they approached the altar our dear Lady Mary came and gave him Our Lord's Body before they reached the altar and he was in great grace as the other seven received the host. And as he ate it, it seemed to him that his cheeks were becoming so big that they would cover over his mouth and it was so sweet that he could not say anything about it except that it was so beyond all sweetness that nobody in the world could speak of it. And the more he chewed the sweeter it was to him. When he came to himself he went to the novice master who was also his father confessor and confessed to him and told him what had happened to him as was written above. And he asked him whether this was right and how long he would have the sweetness—because the father confessor was a wise and learned man. He answered him and said, "Thank God for the great grace that he has given you. I believe that the sweetness will last until the third day." Then he thought. "I trust in God and in his dear mother Mary who has been given to me undeservedly out of true love up to my death. And when he came to table he thought, "If I should eat earthly food this sweetness will be taken away from me and if I refrain from eating today I will be less able to serve God when I get sick. I will eat just a little for the praise of God." And he ate. And while he was eating he no longer had the divine sweetness. Because of this he was very upset and concerned because this grace of God was taken from him. And he ate just a little and then stopped eating. And immediately when he stopped eating he had the divine sweetness from God's grace again internally and externally in all his members just as he had it before and this continued for seventeen years and he never lost it although sometimes he had it more than at other times, more while among the people than at other times.) Our Beloved Lord Jesus Christ showed his love to him and did wonders with him. For that may he be praised forever! The honor is his, he gives it to whomever he wills.

71. One night while she lay in her cell, innumerable evil spirits came and lifted her up to the choir empore and whirled around her and made as if they would pull her apart.²⁴⁶ And they all shrieked and screamed with loud voices, "You wretch, you have taken away from us one who had already been ours body and soul! Since we can not avenge ourselves on you, we want to arrange it so that someone in the monastery will accuse you of lying." Then she made the sign of the holy cross and said, "Go away, you evil spirits! I trust in God completely to protect me from you and your lies." Afterward she took sick and the nuns reviled her and did evil against her, both her relatives and the others as well. They treated her for an illness that she did not have. One day when she lay in great suffering, she went into the church and stood before a crucifix. She usually prayed before it when she was in great suffering. Among other words that she said to Our Lord, she also said, "Lord, what have I done to them, to all the sisters to make them inflict so many insults and so much distress on me?" Then Our Lord said to her, "Tell me, what had I done to those who martyred me? I had created them and formed them after my own image. Consider what suffering they caused me. Be well, I will make you forget this suffering with myself."

72. One time in Advent, when she was so full of divine grace and sweetness she could scarcely reach her cell with the help of other sisters. And when they had laid her down there she went into ecstasy and it was so painful because of her yearning for her beloved dear Jesus Christ, it seemed that her heart would burst to pieces because of true love for him. When she lay there yearning for her Beloved, two virgins came before her. Then she recognized them well, one was named *Spes* and the other *Caritas*.²⁴⁷ They said to her, "Lady, what is wrong with you that you are so sick? What are you yearning for?" She said, "I am yearning for him who is Lord of all lords and God of all gods, for my only beloved Love, Jesus Christ. If he does not come to me I must die. I am very afraid that he will not come to me and that he does not desire me for his wife because I have angered him much all my days. My sins are so great because

I have never been concerned for one hour with his praise, and my heart and my soul desire him and call out to him when I fear he does not want to come to me. Therefore I must die of painful longing for him." The virgins stood before her and the one called *Caritas* said, "No Lady, do not think so ill of yourself. Think how rich, how high, how noble he is and how full of love he is. Love compelled him to come down from heaven and to take on a human nature and to live for nine months in the womb of a virgin. Love compelled him to be born of the virginal body of the Virgin Mary. The invisible God became visible. The incomprehensible God let himself be wrapped in swaddling clothes. The unknowable God let himself be laid in a crib among animals. The God, whom all angels praise and honor began to cry in his childhood. The God, whom all angels serve, accepted as good what a young virgin did for him. The God, who feeds all who live on earth, was fed by his mother. The God, who is passionless in his Godhead was filled with suffering in his humanity out of love. The God, whom neither heaven nor earth is able to praise in his fullness, let himself be circumcised and let himself be named Jesus. Out of love he let himself be presented in the Temple. He, whom all living things fear, fled into Egypt because of his enemies and was poor out of love. Out of love he suffered hunger and thirst. Out of love he experienced no good day on earth. Out of love he showed mercy to all sinners and forgave them their sins. Out of love he made the sick well and the dead living and performed many diverse miracles. He was often tired from preaching, watching and praying. Out of love he rode humbly on an ass to Jerusalem. Out of love he let himself be sold for thirty pennies. Out of the true love of his godly heart he gave his Holy Body to his disciples on Holy Thursday evening and knew in advance all the disgraceful things that would be done to him. In anguish he sweat blood. Love compelled him to give himself into the hands of his enemies and let himself be martyred in such anguish and need that no one can ponder it. He let himself be led before the judge and let himself be flogged at the pillar and let himself be crowned with thorns. He was condemned to death and carried the cross on his back. Out of love he let himself be nailed to the holy cross and was given vinegar and gall to drink. In bitter martyrdom he died out of love on the holy cross. When he had died out of love, his side was pierced and water and blood flowed out from it. This he gives as a gift to all those who love him. Love him and trust him and you will see him." Whenever she heard any speech about her most beloved Love, she became strong and could raise herself up. One of the virgins stepped to one side and the other to the other side and both led her away powerfully. She lay her head on one of them. And it appeared to her in a vision that she was being led through all the world and when she was amazed at the great number of people in the world, she said, "Be amazed that all these have gone before us! Whom do they seek and where do they wish to go? They will indeed be seeking the Creator of all things." Since the way was so far and long, she lost her strength and fell down in a faint. The virgins who were leading her stood before her and said, "No dear Lady, stand up straight and carry on. Remember the strength of the Lord to whom we want to lead you. He is so strong that everything that lives in heaven and on earth has its strength, possessions and life from him. He is so powerful that no one is able to defy his might. In a brief time he created the heavens and also the earth. He is so wise that his wisdom ordered all things wisely. He is so good that he lowers himself to many great sinners out of his goodness. He is so rich that all in heaven and on earth is his. Therefore conduct yourself well and stand up straight. There is nothing lacking in the Lord. To him we wish to lead you so that you will look upon him as your Beloved." Then she regained her strength and stood upright. They led her further near to the place where the Lord himself dwelt. Then again she lost her strength and said, "I am afraid that you do not want to tell me the truth because this way is so very long and far. The virgins said to her, "Conduct yourself well, we are telling you nothing wrong. You will find a thousand times more grace and sweetness in him than we are able to tell.

Think of the beauty of his face. His face is a thousand times more beautiful than the sun. Just as lightning comes down from the sky so rays of light shine forth from his face. His beauty is beyond all human beauty. His beauty exceeds that of all the saints. His beauty is beyond that of the angels. All that is beautiful in heaven and on earth is nothing when compared to his beauty. Joy beyond all joys have all those who look upon him forever." When she heard about his beauty, she became powerfully strong and in joy she came to the place where the Lord, her Beloved, lived. All the gates were opened to them. With joy they entered the city. It was so wide that she could not see to its end. All the paths in the city were of pure gold. It was so high that they could see no roof above. The city was bathed in bright sunlight which was its roof. In the city she saw a bed that was decorated all around with green velvet. The virgins put her down on the bed. While she was lying on the bed she saw her Lord approaching and he was so beautiful that I had never really heard of his beauty since he was a thousand times more beautiful. His face shone brightly and his light outshone the light that filled the city. He came up to me and his beauty shone into my heart and went through all my limbs. Following him was everything in heaven and on earth. The heavenly Mother Mary was closest to him and those who had served him the most followed next. To the degree that every person had served him, to that same degree they followed after him. All of those who live on earth in Christian faith followed him next. Anyone who loved him and served him followed next. Those who were unbelievers on earth now followed him since he had created them, but these were so far away that he did not see them and they likewise could not see him. If they had become believers he would have received them in his mercy. The Lord now approached the bed. In all his joyous beauty he knelt down before the bed and his face was turned toward mine. I looked up and gazed at him. He was so beautiful that I could not bear it and it seemed to me that my soul would dissolve from true love. He said, "My Beloved!" With the same word that so sweetly came out from his mouth he drew my poor, sinful soul into his Godhead and I can say nothing about this vision except to say that it began when they had begun to sing compline and continued until the next day as Mass was being sung. And when I had come to myself I was not able to pray a single *Ave Maria* because of the love in my heart. That joyous, beautiful face that I had seen illumined me interiorly in my soul for more than four weeks.

73. "Oh dear Lord, help me so that my soul may eternally sing your praise in eternal joy with all the highest praise and praise you for your love and thank you eternally for all the good that you have ever granted me, the poor unworthy and least one, and still give to me every day and will ever give to me according to your mercy in eternal joy so that I must thank you for all the good that you have done for your chosen ones, with eternal praise before you, you Holy Trinity."

74. After that on Christmas I saw Our Lord in the form of a small child and he was the same size and form as when he was born from Our Lady and from his feet to his shoulder he was only nine inches long. And he lay in her lap and was so beautiful and lovable that he could not have been more beautiful. And when she looked upon him and thought about what she should say to him and what she should ask for, but suddenly she saw him no more. Then she thought with a sad heart, he could grant everything to her even when she did not see him, just as well as when she looked upon him.

75. At the same time Our Lady,—the sweet queen Mary—came to her at night while she lay on her bed and she carried her Child in her arms and gave the little Child into her arms on the bed.[248] That was unutterably beautiful and he sucked from her breast and remained with her until the bell for matins was rung and she received such great joy from him that there would be much to tell about it for a long time. As she laughed for a time because of the grace and sweetness, so now she cried from love and grace. "Oh you living God, who could deserve such a thing if you did not want to give it freely out of love?"

76. Such great desire overcame her that she suffered wishing that Our Lord would embrace her in his divine arms and press her to him. This desire she had for more than a year without it ever happening. Often she cried and asked God for it with true sincerity. One night after matins she went into the choir and cried for so long that she thought she could not shed another tear over it. After that she went to her cell and laid down and fell asleep immediately. Then it seemed to her that she was in choir once again. In front of the altar were standing three men. They wore lay clothing and were as similar to one another as could be. And from the three lords came one lord who was so beautiful that he could not be more beautiful. His face shone clear as the sun. Suddenly streaming light and brilliance shone forth from his body through his clothing. She stood in the back of choir and thought, will he approach so that she could speak to him and she thought about what she would ask him. And immediately he came to her and stood in front of her. Then she said, "Tell me, dear Lord, which is the greatest sanctuary on earth?" He said, "It is my Holy Body which is daily consecrated." And he said further, "My Beloved Love," and stretched out his arms, embraced her and pressed her against his divine heart so that she thought she clung to him like wax to a seal. For more than four weeks he remained present in her heart just as she had seen him.

77. One night she dreamt that Our Lord was standing in choir appearing as a youth eighteen years old. She went up to where he stood and embraced him. She was permitted to drink from the wound on his side. Then she awoke and was full of divine love and thanked God profusely.

78. She was sick during one Lent and lay . . . two illnesses . . . and recovered from the second illness on Good Friday . . . and was very bad early on Easter morning as day was breaking, when Our Lord bade her to get up and made her completely healthy from this sickness. She told this to one of her friends who had brought her up. She was very happy about it and thanked the Lord for it.

79. This same woman, who had brought her up, was named Elsbet. She was her cousin and was as faithful to her as if she were her mother. She cared for her up to her seventeenth year.[249] Then she took sick and received the holy sacrament with great reverence. And when it came time for her to die, about midnight, she saw a heavenly light come over her and with this Our Lord Jesus Christ appeared with outstretched arms as on the cross. And with that she understood that she had been devoted to the martyrdom of Our Lord and she also saw Our Lady and the holy angel Gabriel. He had a letter on which was written *Ave Maria* by which she recognized that she had held dear the annunciation of Our Lord. Then she died with a holy end, but soon after she came again to her and among the many things about which she asked, she said, "God is so merciful and did such good for me at my end that, if I had known this, I would never have had such great anxiety about my death."

80. Our Lady's Day in Lent fell once on Good Friday and had to be celebrated on the vigil of Palm Sunday.[250] And after matins in a ghostly vision she saw ten sisters from her monastery who had died the same year. For each pair she saw the same reward that they would win before God in eternal joy. One of these was her cousin. She took note of her especially more than the others because she wore the most beautiful attire she had ever seen. She had on a mantle that shone of gold. Beneath the mantle she had on a dress of green velvet interwoven with gold, but was a thousand times more beautiful. She had on two shoes decorated with precious stones and on her head she had a crown that was wondrously beautiful. On her front was a clasp that was so wide that it reached from one arm to the other and covered her chest from her throat down to her lap and in the middle it was as clear as a mirror and all around it went two rows set with colored precious stones. And when she saw this wondrous finery she wondered who this was and asked, "Who is this virgin?" Then she said "It is I, Elsbet." Then she said, "Oh dear one, tell me, are you in heaven?" Then she said, "No." She was given to understand that all ten would be going there

together. The beautiful shoes that she wore meant that she always went quickly to the choir. She was also given to understand, the green dress symbolizes the humility that she possessed. The golden mantle means that she had not liked going to choir, but had done it in true faithfulness under obedience. The crown that she wore meant that she was a pure maiden by nature. The clasp that she wore on the front, with manifold precious stones signified the meaning of the order to which she had belonged and all the good works that she had ever done. In the mirror of the clasp was seen the true purity of her heart and all the suffering she had endured either in secret or in public.

81. Someone was drawn by the grace of God into divine love and sweetness that was incomprehensible and unknown to her.[251] Her spiritual sense was opened up for her and she came to know that Our Lord Jesus Christ was revealing something to her and he said, "Come here, my Beloved, my Love and my Tender One, and kiss the wound of my right hand and draw out from it my divine mercy because for this I was wounded on the cross so that I would be mild and merciful to you since to him whose hands were pierced nothing can be denied.[252] I will share with you my mercy and mildness forever. Come here, my Love and kiss my left hand and draw from it my obedience which I have shown to my heavenly Father unto death and the obedience which all my friends have shown to me in both religious and secular life from the beginning of the world and still show me until Judgment Day, so that I give it to you as completely as if you yourself had given me obedience in true love. Come here, my Faithful One and kiss my right foot and draw from it divine faithfulness and forget with me all the infidelity that others have ever shown to you and also the suffering that has come to you in your most beloved friend, whom I have taken away from you. Conduct yourself well for I wish to take care of you now and forever and be concerned with everything that is necessary for your body and soul. Come here, my Pure One, and kiss my left foot and draw from it the divine

purity of my Godhead and my Manhood and all the purity that my mother had ever won and all the saints and angels and humans on earth from the beginning until Judgment Day in order that I give it to you in true love as if you had always lived in purity as they had so that you will be pure even now and forever. And draw out from my left foot so that I may protect you from evil spirits so that they can never harm you in body or soul now or ever. Now come here and kiss the wound on my side and draw from it the overflow and receive satisfaction beyond all delight from my divinity and humanity." Then Our Lord Jesus Christ overflowed with tenderness and gave her ten thousand sinners to be converted, ten thousand good people to be confirmed in a good life and ten thousand souls to be delivered from purgatory.

82. As one counts 1,344 years after the birth of Christ on the Friday after the Assumption of Our Lady, the nuns went behind the altar and the laypeople and religious processed with the cross. That was arranged because of the great general interdict which was over holy Christendom.[253] One also said that darkness so great and dreary would come and the crops would rot.[254] And the people fasted on bread and water for three Fridays. That was ordered in all the parishes. On the same three Fridays all processed with the most Blessed Sacrament and the crosses. We processed also with the crosses and with the sacrament in our monastery to our altar and we sang to God and the saints according to our custom and when we returned to the choir we sang the antiphon to our Lady *Beati Dei Genetrix*. Then the heavens were moved and the mother of God stood before God the Son and said, "My Lord and my Son, I ask you to remember that you have given me to sinners for consolation on earth and that I bore you and gave birth to you and gave you suck and I remained a pure virgin, and remember all the good that I ever had shown you and therefore have mercy on the people." St. John the Baptist with all the holy patriarchs and prophets stood before the Holy Trinity and said, "Lord, Ruler over all the world, have mercy on the people." St. John the Evangelist and St. Peter with

all the holy apostles stood before God and said, "You, Ruler over all the earth, have mercy on the people." St. Stephen with all the holy martyrs stood before the Holy Trinity and said, "You, Ruler, over all the earth, have mercy on the people." St. Catherine and St. Ursula with all holy virgins stood before God and all cried out, "You, Lord over all the earth, have mercy on the people." All the angels in heaven and all the saints cried out together, "You, Ruler over all the earth, have mercy on the people." Our beloved Love and our Spouse, our Lord Jesus Christ stood before his heavenly Father and showed him the five wounds that he had received from us, and these now shone in such clarity that no one could describe them. He said, "Loving Father, have mercy on the people. I have not bought them with silver or gold, I have bought them with the blood that was in my human nature." Then the Father in heaven spoke sweetly, "I will have mercy on them and will give them good years." And he commanded the angels who were responsible for the heavens and the firmament to direct it along the right course so that the darkness and starvation would not come so that there would be good years. He said to God the Son, "What do you want to give them?" Then he said, "All those who have followed after me without mortal sin and who have prayed to me will gain eternal life." He said to the Holy Spirit, "What will you give them?" Then the Holy Spirit said, "To those who are still in mortal sins I will give recognition of their sins and real repentance for them in their last hour so that they may stand before me." You who hear or read this should know that by this is meant all those who process with the cross whether religious or lay.

83. To her was also made known that the world in general had not prayed fervently enough and therefore was visited with these years of famine so that all the living would lament over themselves or their friends. God also revealed to her that if the people had concerned themselves as much with the interdict as with the darkness he would have brought it to an end. However, it lasted many a year. She experienced this spiritually and not

bodily because she acknowledged that she rarely saw things with her bodily eyes.

84. One time a priest, named Brother Berchtold of Moosburg, was saying Mass.[255] Then she saw with her bodily eyes that he received Our Lord and that Our Lord stood at the altar in the form of that priest and she saw the priest no more and he gave the monastery the blessing. She was scarcely able to refrain from crying out with a loud voice.

85. Once the prioress had asked the sister to leave the monastery with her because the monastery was in grave need.[256] Then she thought about what the Lord's will would be and one morning when she was at prayer she saw our Lady sitting by her. She was wondrously beautiful and held our Lord sitting on her lap. He was a child of about three years and he had a wreath of red and white roses on his head. And when she saw our Lord and our Lady sitting there she thought to herself, "That is a sign that you will remain here at home."[257] The monastery fell into such need that the nuns wanted to leave the monastery. She opposed that whenever she heard it. This caused her great suffering and she thought, "Oh Lord, even if nothing happens to the sisters I will always grieve." She thought this because she had spoken about the Faithful One that they had in God.

86. As she lay in suffering on a Sunday during the time for Mass, Our Lord appeared to her as he had been at thirty years of age and said that nothing would happen to them neither on the farm nor in the cloister "as long as you remain here." Then she was so happy about this that she told it to her good friends. The danger was so great that they were threatened with the burning of the monastery and the theft of the animals. However no harm came to them either in the monastery or on the farm just as Our Beloved Lord Jesus Christ had foretold it.

87. On St. Louis Day she was distressed about gossip that she had heard concerning the monastery.[258] When the Mass *Gaudeamus* was being sung she was enraptured in divine union with Our Lord

Jesus Christ.[259] He let her recognize him as the sun and said, "I am the sun that shines over mountains and valleys. Also I appear to all human hearts and nothing is hidden from me. All thoughts, both evil and good, are known to me. You should not be distressed on account of the monastery. I will never let it vanish and those who remain in it out of love and do not leave the monastery I will confirm my love in them. And those who have entered out of fear, I will take away their evil fear before their death and will give them eternal love. You should know that all who leave the monastery bring harm to religious people. When they return home again they receive a shock from the world. What they have seen and heard effects them often. Illicit sex and leaving the monastery are the same. Oh how richly will I give the rich treasures of my divinity to those who give it up for my sake! Here below and later eternally they will enjoy me!" He said to her, "I will grant everything for which you pray from now until your death. Whatever you pray for earnestly I will grant you. Of all those whom you commend to me in your prayers none will ever be parted from me. And to all humans to whom you speak I will inflame with my love more than before. And of all those born into your family none will ever be separated from me." Then he said to the angels—the Cherubim and Seraphim and called upon the nine choirs of angels, "You should watch over my friend so that all her thoughts at all times should be directed to me so that her heart may feel here how it burns in my love."

88. During the night before the day when she would make her profession many devils came and brought a wagon and said, "Come with us! You should go to hell with us! You do not belong in the kingdom of heaven."[260] Then she said, "Away with you, you evil wretches! I trust in my Lord Jesus Christ. He will never let me be parted from him." Then they screamed so loudly and made such a noise that she became so ill from it that she could not utter another word, thinking she would die from such distress. So little strength was left in her that she could not lift her hand to make the sign of the cross. So she made a cross in her mouth with her

tongue. She thought to herself, "If only I could cry out, I would call out so that people would come to me." After that she thought, "No, Lord, I swear that if you wish it of me I will suffer this up to my death. But only do not leave me!" Immediately after that she lost consciousness. Then angels came ever closer to her and many of them played harps, but most of them blew shawms. The holy angels drove the devils away. The angels floated up to the windows in the cloister and were as bright as the sun and they played their shawms and their playing was sweeter than any music she had ever heard. She went into the chapter room and in the prioress' place sat a lord who wore the most beautiful attire. It went beyond what one could imagine. The color resembled the daffodils in May. On the cloth sparkled innumerable little golden stars and his face shone like the sun. She knelt down before him and he received her vows. When she had promised him obedience, he embraced her in his arms and enclosed her in his cloak and pressed her lovingly against his heart and said, "May you be well, my beloved child and do not fear for I will never abandon you." And she believed him to be her dear lord, St. Dominic.

89. Once on the feast of St. Thomas the Preacher when she got up in the morning, St. Thomas was standing in front of her and his face was wonderfully beautiful.[261] His habit and his tunic were white as the snow. His cappa was beautiful beyond all measure and on front over his heart was the Holy Trinity. It was so beautiful that it filled the cell with light. My lord, St. Thomas said, "When I was on earth I carried the Holy Trinity at all times in my heart and when I grew old I let it be painted and sewed it on my habit. Whenever anyone did me honor I gave it to the Holy Trinity." Just then the bell for prime was rung and she went to choir.

90. She had an aunt who was a very worldly woman and a young and beautiful widow. She sent to her to pray to Our Lord for her to know what course she should take in life. She prayed to Our Lord more than four weeks. Then Our Lord said, "If she renounces the world for my sake and becomes a religious I will forgive her all her

sins and will make her good. If she does not do this I will shorten her days and give her severe penances." She wrote this to her from our dear Lord. Then she said, "I do not want to become a nun. I want to take a husband. It is not true that Our Lord will shorten my days." She took a wealthy husband. Immediately she took sick during the first four weeks. Then she sent for her friends and said to them, "I know for sure I will die. If I had followed God, he would not have shortened my days." She died from the same sickness and was put into the penance and pain of purgatory.

91. On All Saints Day she was led by the spirit into purgatory and she saw the souls there in all sorts of suffering.[262] There she was also led to those souls who had already done penance for everything but still did not yet see God. There she saw various sisters from her monastery, who were thought to be already above in heaven, but were not yet there.[263] She saw the soul of her mother among them. She too was thought to have already reached heaven a long time ago. She saw innumerable souls there. If just one *Ave Maria* or a *Pater Noster* or *Miserere* were to be said for them they would go immediately to heaven. They had no other pain except that they could not yet see God. After that it was so lamentable for them that they all cried out, "Lord, have mercy on us and give someone to help us. It has been said that we are already in heaven and no one prays for us." They all cried out, "Lord, mighty God, give this one the same pain that we suffer, as long as she stays here with us so that she will pray for us more willingly." Immediately the same pain was given to her. She suffered from such thirst that it seemed to her she would certainly die at this time from thirst. Her thirst was not for bodily drink, it was for God and for the joys of heaven and for the *Ave Maria*. And she also cried out with them, "Lord, have mercy on us and rouse up our friends to help us." She cried out loudly, "You, all dear friends, even those for whom I have never done anything good, have mercy on me and help me out of my distress." In purgatory when an *Ave Maria* was recited for someone it benefited all other souls and all became happy like when someone who is very

thirsty is given a drink of water. When she came to herself again she helped many souls whom she had recognized—two souls especially. She prayed for them now more gladly than before because she knew their suffering well and thanked Our Lord because he had not abandoned her to the fires of purgatory.

92. She had a companion named Jutta Pfinzing, who was very dear to her.[264] She became prioress on the ninth day after St. Michael Day on the feast of the holy Pope Mark.[265] And when she made her venia she [was tempted to believe that the devil possessed her and she had to act very foolishly and could neither speak nor point. She would have given all the world to have this suffering be removed from her and] (had such a severe temptation that she would have given the entire world not to have. And she was so strange that . . .) everyone who saw this believed that she had lost all her senses.[266] The whole monastery was very distressed about this, especially about this sister. She took her cause on before God with great diligence. And on All Saints Day she saw in spirit how the devil was leading the prioress by the hand.[267] The devil was very tall and big and led her so forcefully that it seemed he would never let her go. And when she saw that he was leading the prioress around she said, "You evil spirit! By the living God I order you to stand still!" He acted very defiantly as if he wanted to lead her away. Then she said, "I order you by the Father and the Son and the Holy Spirit and by the Last Judgment to stand still and not lead her away! You, evil fiend! She has already been God's handmaiden from her childhood. What do you have to do with her?" Then he screeched. She began to be in pain. After the prioress' installation she said, "Be gone! Go away! I command you by God!" Then she prayed to Our Lord with great earnestness for him to remove the sufferings of the prioress. Then Our Lord said, "I deliver her from her suffering to you so that from now on until her death no such suffering will ever befall her." Immediately she went to the prioress and asked her how she was. She answered, "I am well. This night from the time of matins my suffering has been taken away from

me." At that same time she had prayed to God for her. The prioress thanked God and her with tear-filled eyes, as well she might since she had been saved from great suffering.

93. On St. Matthew Day the sisters received Our Lord in communion and when she had received Our Lord he was good to her beyond all measure.[268] She was amazed about that and wondered why he was so good to her since she certainly had not deserved it. Then God answered her, "Why are you wondering? Augustine was a great sinner yet I converted him and made of him a renowned teacher of Holy Scripture and a great saint. And Mary of Egypt was a public sinner yet I made of her a great saint."[269] After that she was out of herself and did not know what good God did for her. When she came to herself again her soul spoke of Our Lord Jesus Christ. "He looked upon me with the eyes of his mercy and his eyes were full of love."

The *Prayer* of Adelheid Langmann

94. I remind you, Holy Trinity, of all the crying and calling out raised up to you by the fathers of old in ancient times until you became man on earth and of all the crying out and yearning that all people directed to you from the beginning of the world and will ever direct to you up to the Judgment Day in love and suffering, sorrow and joy—how they have called out to you for your love and your mercy. I ask you, Lord, to receive all these cries and voices as if they arose from my own mouth. I want to gather all the voices of all the yearning hearts ever raised up to you from the beginning of the world and all that will ever be raised up to you up to Judgment Day in heaven and also on earth. They must all come forth from my mouth and you rich God, you mighty God, you immortal God, you loving God, you faithful God, you merciful God, give a favorable hearing so that you will come into my heart and fill me up completely with your love and all your grace and take away from me all my sins and help me to live a holy and perfect life so that I will be found in that state on my last day.

95. I remind you, Lord, of the intention that you have in your eternal Godhead, you Eternal Father in heaven with your Eternal Son and with the Holy Spirit, to save the human race from everlasting death and how you, out of your paternal favor, gave your only-begotten Son to become man and how you, Lord Eternal Son, offered your divine will to that and how you, Lord Holy Spirit, gave

your divine goodness to that and how you chose the Virgin Mary from all women for that and how you sent your angel to deliver the message. And I ask you, Lord, to turn your paternal favor toward me and give me your only-begotten Son as my eternal consolation and my eternal reward here now and later in eternity. May your Eternal Son turn toward me according to your divine will and be my eternal Bridegroom, so that you, Lord, and I will never be parted from each other neither here nor in eternity. May you, Lord Holy Spirit, inflame me with the fire of your love so that my heart must burst more from love than from the pain of death.

96. I remind you that the angel came through the locked door to the Virgin Mary and ask you to lock up my heart against all evil and direct my senses to your all-highest praise.[270]

97. I remind you that the all-holiest Virgin Mary was in deep reverence at prayer and ask you to give me perfect reverence and divine love in all my praying and in all my life.

98. I remind you, Lord, that the angel found her perfect in holiness and that you had sanctified her so that she was without sin because she was always overflowing with all grace. And so I ask you to bring me to all perfection and fill me up with all graces so that nothing will be lacking in me and you will find me ready at all times when you come.

99. I remind you, Lord, of the love that you bore for her when the angel greeted her as a righteous woman and announced to her that she should be your mother and how she said, "How can that be for I do not know a man?"[271] Lord, I remind you that she was, even in her early days, a seeker after your hidden mysteries who wanted to know the truth. I ask you, Lord, to let me recognize the real truth without any misconceptions in all divine things and may I also receive your grace according to your dearest will to seek to please no one but you alone.

100. I remind you, Lord, that the angel spoke with joyful words, "Fear not, Mary, you have found favor with God. The Holy Spirit will come upon you and the power of the All-Highest will

overshadow you."²⁷² I ask you, Lord, to give me loving fear and divine determination to serve you in real truth and true love and with unwavering diligence forever. And you, Holy Spirit, come into me and help me to obtain all virtues and every good thing according to your dearest will and to your highest praise so that I will be found so on my last day.

101. I remind you, Lord, of the humble, loving and sweet reply that the pure Virgin gave. "I am the humble handmaiden of God, let it happen to me according to your word."²⁷³ Lord, I ask you to give me perfect humility so that, with all your graces, I remain loving and humble.

102. I remind you, Lord, that when she spoke this word, you became true God and true Man in that hour in her womb, just as mighty, as good, and as powerful as you are in heaven and yet you became a little child, body and soul, God and Man together. I ask you, Lord, by that same love, to fill up my soul, my body and all my senses with the abundance of your mercy, of your divinity and of your humanity so that all my thoughts, my words, my deeds, my will and the way of my whole life be godly and always be pleasing in your sight.

103. I remind you, Lord, that she carried you nine months in her womb and remind you of all the grace and sweetness that you showed to her while you were in her body: make my whole life pleasing to you.

104. I remind you of the visit that your mother made to St. Elizabeth and how St. John was made holy in his mother's womb, and ask you, Lord, to make me holy in real truth.²⁷⁴

105. I remind you, Lord, of the love your dear mother possessed as she carried you, true God and true Man, beneath her heart and how she often said with great joy, "My Lord, my Creator, my God, my Joy, me Delight, my Consolation, when will come the day, the hour, the time when my eyes will look upon you?" O my most beloved Love, help me so that after this suffering I may see you with joy in eternal joy. O my tender Lord, help me so that I may enjoy you in joy eternally, after this suffering, by all the love and the care

that your mother ever gave you and by the service all angels and saints and peoples on earth have ever given you and will ever give to you up to Judgment Day by your goodness. Do hear my prayer now.

106. I remind you that you were born of her virginal, pure womb as true God and true Man and ask you to bring about the spiritual birth within me so that you will be born spiritually from my soul by your eternal love.

107. I remind you that you were surrounded with heavenly light and with all graces and ask you to illuminate my soul with your divine light and with all graces.

108. I remind you, Lord, of all the joys that your mother shared when she enjoyed her first sight of you and remind you of the joys that you had when you returned her gaze with your human eyes since you had chosen her from all women. And I ask you, Lord, by your birth and for the sake of this gaze to look upon me with the eyes of your mercy so that when my soul departs from my mouth and is drawn by sight into your Godhead and is led to it, that it have eternal joy with you by the loving sight with which you looked upon your mother, all angels and all saints in eternal joy.

109. I remind you, Lord, that your mother was the first to worship you in Christian faith and ask you to grant me Christian faith and Christian works forever.

110. I remind you that she kissed you on your sweet mouth as a firm reconciliation of your divinity with your humanity and I ask you to bring all my unrest to a sure reconciliation in you.

111. I remind you that you were wrapped in a weak and poor towel and ask you to wrap yourself up in my poor, unworthy heart and in my soul.[275]

112. I remind you, that you were laid in a crib with animals and that they knelt before you and worshiped you, my Lord and my God, and I ask you to remove all my animal-like behavior and give me true, firm faithfulness and recognition of you.

113. I remind you, Lord, that the blacksmith nearby was already making the nails with which you would be nailed to the Holy Cross

and that the hammering already rang in your infant ears and I ask you, Lord, by your Holy Childhood to forgive me if I have ever offended you from the days of my childhood to the present day.

114. I remind you, Lord, that the angels announced your birth to the shepherds in the field so that they would come to find and worship you.[276] I ask you to help me to worship you in real truth so that you will never be taken from me.

115. I remind you that you were circumcised and that you shed your child's blood and I ask you to cleanse me from all my sins.[277]

116. I remind you that you cried and ask you to give me sweet tears of love for all my sins.

117. I remind you that you were given the name Jesus, the healer, and I ask you to heal me inwardly and outwardly in soul and in body, in heart and senses and spirit, for you know all that brings me into confusion.

118. I remind you that you revealed your birth to the Three Kings by various signs and that they prepared themselves to search for you with all the love of their hearts and I ask you to give me complete readiness so that you will always find me ready at your coming.[278]

119. I remind you that you guided and led them by the star and I ask you to guide me with love and not with suffering since you know all about my sickness.[279]

120. I remind you that they offered you myrrh and frankincense and gold and I ask you to give me myrrh—remorse for my sins and compassion with your martyrdom; frankincense—true, reverent prayer and true Christian belief; and gold—divine love and Christian works.[280]

121. I remind you that you received their offerings and ask you to receive my soul when it departs from my mouth and lead it yourself into eternal joy.

122. I remind you of the good deed when she nursed you and gave you to eat and drink, picked you up and bathed you and I ask you to forgive me whenever I took too much care with my body in eating, drinking, sleeping and clothing and

all the luxuries I allowed my body and the good things I have ever done to my body.

123. I remind you, Lord, of the joy when she carried you up to the Temple, how she took you in her arms, my Lord and my God, and her dear Son, with two turtledoves in her apron to offer them in the Temple, and that the lord Simeon took you in his arms and that he prophesied about you and you illumined him inwardly and outwardly.[281] And I ask you, Lord, to illumine my soul with your holy Divinity and with your holy Humanity and make known to me the hidden secrets of your sweetness so that I may enjoy them here below in true mercy, in true love, and there above in eternity may see them in full joy and enjoy them and praise you without ceasing, without end.

124. I remind you, Lord, of the sorrow that your dear mother felt when the lord Simeon prophesied that because of your saving power a sharp sword would pierce her heart and because of this she was so distressed and cried bitterly because she knew your future.[282] I ask you, living God, by your great mercy to protect me and shield me from future misery and suffering in body and soul, in senses and in spirit, me and my friends as well. And protect us from curses and prayers for our death, me and my friends.

125. I remind you, Lord, of the children who were killed for your sake and ask you to kill all my sins with love and not with suffering.[283]

126. I remind you, Lord, that the angel made known to Joseph while he slept, that he should flee into Egypt and that your dear mother took you, my Lord and my God, her dear Son, and fled with Joseph into Egypt.[284] I ask you, Lord, to remember all your mercifulness. Since you know all things, you know well that I, Lord, have fled to you in this monastery in true faith and ask you to help me to win the victory over the devil, the world and my own body.

127. I remind you of the loving guidance and home that your mother and Joseph gave you in the foreign land of Egypt and I ask you to help me so to live with my friends that it will praise and honor you and be of assistance to me.

128. I remind you, Lord, of the shelter you found along the way in foreign lands and I ask you, after this suffering, to give me shelter with you in your kingdom.

129. I remind you, Lord, that at your arrival in Egypt all the idols fell down and were shattered and I ask you, Lord, to drive away all evil spirits from me so that they will never gain any control over me nor possess me neither here in this life nor at the hour of my death nor after this life in any way at all.

130. I remind you that you were in Egypt for seven years and I ask you to forgive me whenever I have offended you with the seven capital sins and with all sins that I have committed against you. Give me the seven gifts of the Holy Spirit and cleanse me thoroughly from my sins so that I will become as pure as when I was lifted up from the waters of baptism. For that I will gladly suffer bodily death.

131. I remind you that after seven years Herod died and I ask you to lay all my enemies, whether visible or invisible, before my feet so that they will never do me any harm and their cursing and prayers for my death will harm neither me nor my friends.

132. I remind you that you were led home to the Holy Land and were received lovingly and happily by all your friends and I ask you to sanctify me with yourself and receive me in the peace of your eternal mercy.

133. I remind you that she, your mother, lost you, for three days.[285] Lord. Whenever I lose you, help me to find you.

134. I remind you that you taught the Jews for three days in the Temple and ask you to teach me in this life to accomplish all divine things according to your dearest will so that you will teach me repentance and pure perfect contrition at my end.[286] And give me your Holy Body as food that will remain with me forever and the holy oil and all Christian things so that my heart will burst within me more out of love for you than from the pain of death. Teach me to enjoy you after this life and to praise you in eternal joy in the all-greatest joys and with your most-beloved friends to enjoy and praise you without ceasing, without end.

135. I remind you that your dear mother found you in the Temple and rejoiced in her heart and soul and I ask you to give me joy and to grant me everything for which I have prayed.[287]

136. I remind you, Lord, of all the good and holy deeds that you ever did in your holy childhood and ask you to forgive me for all the evil deeds that I ever did in my childhood and throughout my life.

137. I remind you, Lord, that you were baptized in the Jordan and I ask you to baptize me in the love of the Holy Spirit so that I will turn away from all my sins.[288]

138. I remind you, Lord, that John had you in his hands and heard the voice of the Father when he said, "This is my Beloved Son, on whom my favor rests."[289] And he saw the Holy Spirit in the form of a dove. I ask you to bring me into the mysteries of your Divinity and make known to me your divine mercy and help me to persevere in all your graces as it is pleasing to your fatherly heart.

139. I remind you that you fasted forty days and forty nights in the wilderness and that you took neither food nor drink.[290] I ask you to make me able to fast, to watch, to pray and to meditate, to accomplish all divine things according to your dearest will.

140. I remind you that you were tempted and tried by the evil spirit and ask you to help me to withstand all his temptations and trials.[291]

141. I remind you that you changed water into wine at the wedding feast and began to perform signs publicly.[292] I ask you to work wonderfully your mercy in me and give me to drink and make me drunk with the Cyprian wine of your sweet Divinity.[293]

142. I remind you, Lord, that because of her repentant tears and her burning zeal when she washed your feet with her tears and dried them with her hair, you forgave Mary Magdalene all her sins and set her on the course of a contemplative life.[294] I ask, Lord, by all the love that your good and loving heart showed to her and always has shown to everyone who loves you, to forgive me all my sins and set me on the way to a contemplative life and draw me into the mirror of your tender Divinity so that you will

be at all times and in every hour in my soul and in my heart and that there be nothing below you to lead my heart astray, that I leave all that is against you and that I accomplish everything that is your dearest will.

143. I remind you that you gave recognition of all her sins to the heathen woman at the well and I ask you to let me recognize all my sins and failings and give me total contrition for them.[295]

144. I remind you of the woman brought before you who had committed adultery and that she was accused of her sin before you and that you, good God, were merciful to her.[296] I ask you, dear Lord, to remember your mercifulness when I am accused before you every day. Now the world accuses me because I follow its ways too much and pursue its cares too much. Now my body accuses me because I am too good to it and treat it tenderly. The evil spirit accuses me because I do not resist his evil counsel and his temptations. O tender, sweet Lord, I now stand before you like a guilty criminal before the judge, not knowing whether he will pardon or condemn him. Oh! Dear Lord! All my evil thoughts lie open before you and my evil words and deeds. Now I can hide nothing from you. Tender Lord, today I give myself over to your divine, boundless mercy and to the divine flames of your burning love so that you can melt and burn up all my sins in it. Lord, do not damn me in your anger and do not cast me away in your justice. Draw me to you with love and fill me with all your graces.

145. I remind you, Lord, of all your good words, of all your good works and of all your holy thoughts. Lord, they make up today for all my sins.

146. I remind you, Lord, of your pure life, your holy way of life. May it make up today for all that I have ever done against you.

147. I remind you, Lord, of how tired you became from preaching, fasting, crying and praying. I offer that up to your heavenly Father today for all my sins. Be reconciled to me today so that there will be nothing between me and you.

148. I remind you of all the holy signs that you performed on earth, that you made the dead to live and the blind to see and the crooked straight and the leper clean. I ask you, Lord, to grant a divine sign to me, poor sinner, and give me a perfect life so that I will be found perfect in my last days.

149. I remind you, Lord, that you were on earth for thirty-three years and that you never had a good day, and ask you to make my whole life acceptable in your eyes.

150. I remind you, Lord, that you rode up to Jerusalem on a humble little animal, on a donkey, and that the crowds of this world ran to meet you and gave you great honor by taking off their garments and laying them at your feet and they broke palm branches and strew them before you to honor you and they received you and praised you in song and gave you all the honor they could give.[297] I ask you, Lord, when you come into the Jerusalem of my heart and soul, to give me such readiness for you so that you will always find me ready to give you true honor with body, soul, heart, senses and spirit.

151. I remind you, Lord, that you preached through the whole day and into the night and went away still fasting and no one gave you anything to eat or drink. I ask you, Lord, when you come to my soul, that I may give you true love to eat so that you will remain with me forever.

152. I remind you, that you were betrayed.[298] Lord, whenever I have betrayed you and whenever I have spoken against you, forgive me.

153. I remind you, Lord, that you were sold for thirty pennies and I ask you never to let me gain either goods or friends, who are so dear to me that I forget you.[299]

154. I remind you that you taught your disciples on Holy Thursday and preached to them and made them wise—and enlightened them—in faith and real truth.[300] I ask you, Lord, to be my faithful teacher and guide me to do your will and to hold to your commands.

155. I remind you, Lord, of the love that you had when you gave us your Holy Body on Holy Thursday and ask you to give me true, perfect love to receive your Holy Body so that I may conceive you spiritually even as your mother conceived you bodily when you were announced by the angel St. Gabriel.

Excerpts of Correspondence

Adelheid Langmann and Ulrich of Kaisheim

156. Then this sister asked one of her religious friends, who was a specially chosen friend of Our Lord Jesus Christ and was prior of Kaisheim to pray for her to Our Lord.[301] She often asked this of him with great earnestness. Once while he was saying Mass, during the Mass and afterward, he prayed for her with great earnestness. Our Lord Jesus Christ said to him with true love and sweetness, "I will pour my heart into her heart and her heart into my heart and will unite them together and will care for both. She should not grieve over anything. When I go away from her and she thinks she has lost me, I am in her soul sleeping and resting in it and preparing for myself a place in her and for her in me. When she looks for me, she will find me within herself. Therefore she should not be distressed about anything, rather she should be untroubled about all things. We are united and are one thing."—"Lord, what will you give us for a dowry?" Then Our Lord Jesus Christ said, "For that I will give all the treasures that I brought from my Father in heaven to earth—my Divinity and my Humanity." Then the person said, "Lord, how will you prepare a place for us with you?" The Lord said, "I will prepare the best place and not a common one. I have bound both of you to me with the bands of the Holy Trinity. I have united both of you to me in the unity of the Holy Trinity. I have made both of you of one mind in the unanimity of the Holy Trinity. Both of you will be given the gift of the Holy Trinity. Both are powerful with the

power of the Holy Trinity. Both of you are wise in the wisdom of the Holy Trinity. You are loved in the love of the Holy Trinity. You are sweet in the sweetness of the Holy Trinity. You are rich in the riches of the Holy Trinity. You are noble in the nobility of the Holy Trinity. Amen."

157. After Mass on St. Matthew Day before the altar of St. John:[302] "My heart is open and unlocked to both of you this evening and morning. The evening is all of this life. The morning is the rising to eternal life. Nevermore, now or hereafter, will it be locked to you. From this I will grant you to know whatever you wish. You, yourselves, should take whatever you want and desire and also for whomever you wish, assuredly and quickly, for this is so incomprehensibly more than whatever has yet been given you and will be given to you in time and in eternity. This is so beyond all telling that no one could tell about it. You are enclosed here and forever in the mercy of my heart so that nothing will be able to separate you here and there in eternity and you can tell this to whomever you will. Amen. This is what Our Lord announced to this sister through the priest.

158. "Tell me, dear Lord, how do you like what she recommended?" Then Our Lord said, "That seems right to me, like someone who has a true, heartfelt, only love and who does not gladly see anything disagreeable in him. Therefore I will protect her from all offensive things. Amen.

159. She was in great suffering and asked the same man to write something to her.[303] So he wrote her this: "You are loved by your Bridegroom, totally loved from the heart. He protects you and will not cease to protect you. He has the honor of your suffering and you have the reward. He provokes him with you.[304] He will not let you be defeated. He will not leave you wanting in the little bridal bed for a time. He protects your humility. He wants you to show mercy to the poor. He lets you be hunted and driven towards him so that you will serve him more fervently. Just as without shame a bride falls upon her bridegroom, caresses his neck, embraces him,

kisses him and presses against him—see, that is his intention. He adorns you and arrays you with flowers according to the delight of his own good pleasure. He plays a game of love with you yet never has enough. He makes himself dear to you at every hour and at all times with true devotion and with new graces since he is most pleasing to you and you to him. He cools his love with you. With you he forgets all the suffering that happens to him from other people. He has become uncontrollable toward you out of love and wants to have praise and honor before his friends and is ashamed of nothing before his enemies. In brief, he has become drunk with love and behaves toward you like a child. Therefore, ask and command him immediately. Whatever you want, he wants and whatever he will not grant to you according to his will, he will give you something much better. Often he will act as if to play at betraying you and wanting to abandon you or to drive you away. Pay no heed. Believe me, it is his intention for you to act more tenderly and kindly. It is over with me. But it has only begun with him and you. May God be honored!"

160. This same person was in ecstasy and invited to the cradle of the pure, chaste Virgin Mary.[305] There she was given the greeting by the mother of the Child with these words, "Greet him from me with all the love and all the goodness that was given to me with my Child from the heavenly Father without pain."—"Oh Lady, for that I am totally prepared." Then our dear Lady said, "And give him yet another greeting—with all the good that flows from all pure hearts to me and also with all that flows from the Holy Trinity to me."—"This greeting was given to me and I send it to you." Then the soul was also shown a tree with blossoms of such a kind that no one could ever see more beautiful blossoms. The tree bore as many blossoms as it could bear and also on the tree was all the good that it could bear. And the one gives the tree to the other in the cradle: the Mother to the Child and the Child to the Mother as a gift. And our Lady gave me this tree as a Christmas present and told me to send it to you. God be honored!"

161. [306]"The fruitful power—that is there from the divine nature in the Father's heart, in this power and by this power the Virgin Mary was made pregnant with the eternal Word by the power, the working and overshadowing of the Holy Spirit, and from which power she took her fruitfulness and takes it still—this same power is sent to you, to make your thoughts, words and works fruitful. You should share this power with all human beings and especially you should bear all sinful hearts in this power so that they will be made righteous by it, and all languid hearts to be set on the right path and all withered hearts so that they become green and all blossoming hearts that they may bear ripe fruit and all greening hearts that they may blossom. You should receive this power so that you may obtain a special virtue from every person. This is sent to you for this reason: during the course of your life one sin has given birth to another, but now a virtue gives birth to others in you. From this you should receive awareness of yourself (that is you should become aware that up to now you have worked against God and this awareness should lead you to a divine awareness far more profound than you have ever had) and then gentleness and patience in all trials and firm opposition and constant courage in everything that happens to you, and a passionate, fiery love in which all your sins will disappear and in which you will be given a new life and a sweet dialogue of your soul with God more than before, in which you will receive more divine sweetness than ever before and on that basis perfect humility too,—and also constant diligence in that you accomplish these things and receive within a loving heart for all. You should also know that the efficacious power is a preparation for the fruitful power and should also prepare you to be capable of and receptive to the joyous power. God be honored!

162. I did not understand that very well. Then our Lord came and explained it. "I, the Eternal Father in heaven, brought forth my only-begotten Son. Of that birth no one, neither angel nor human, can speak about or explain, and through him I have made all things pregnant and fruitful. There has never yet been a sinner so great

that when I forgave him his sin I forgave him so completely as if he had never committed a sin, then he improves himself totally and never again commits a sin. As my dear Mother lovingly gave birth to me, so such a person gives birth to me spiritually in true love so that I place within him my divine grace and the sweetness of my divine consolation. The heart, that was formerly cast down, is made just again. The heart that was formerly withered becomes green. The heart that was formerly unloving acquires love and blossoms and I bring it to perfect fruitfulness. The same person should then pray to me for other sinners who are still in sin and should bear the sin for me with a full heart as if he himself were in sin. Because no one can do anything more dear to me than to pray for sinners. Amen."

Select Bibliography

Manuscripts of Die Offenbarungen

B = Berlin, Staatsbibliothek Preussischer Kulturbesitz, mgq 866: 86r-215v
M = München, Staatsbibliothek, cgm 99: 36r-173r.
W = Wien, Bibliothek des Schottenstifts, *Codex Scotensis Vindobonensis* (234): 120r-168r.

Translations

Prestel, Josef. *Die Offenbarungen der Margaretha Ebner und der Adelheid Langmann* Weimar: Verlag Hermann Bohlaus Nachfolger, 1939:113-183.

Buber, Martin. *Ecstatic Confessions.* San Francisco: Harper and Rowe, Publishers, 1985; originally published in German as *Ekstatische Konfessionen.* Jena: Eugen Dietrichs Verlag, 1909; (exerpts - paragraphs 1-5 only).

Secondary Sources

MANUSCRIPTS

United Kingdom

German Manuscript 10, 009, 1559. British Library *Geschlecht-buch der stat Nürnberg*

Germany

Cod. Cent. V 99, Nürnberger Stadtbibliothek, *Das Leben der heiligen Christina Ebnerin*

Cod. Cent. VII 25, Nürnberger Stadtbibliothek, *Anweisungen für die Tischlesungen* (St. Katharina Monastery).

Cod. Cent. VII 79, Nürnberger Stadtbibliothek. *Katalog der Klosterbibliothek* (St. Katharina).

Cod. Cent. VII 92, Nürnberger Stadtbibliothek. *Verzeichnis der Privatbücher der Schwestern* (St. Katharina).

Austria

Codex 2686, Natioanlbibliothek, Vienna.

Codex 2719, Nationalbibliothek, Vienna.

MSC 2759-2764, Nationalbibliothek, Vienna.

Other Secondary Sources

_____. "The Primitive Constitutions of the Monastery of San Sisto." *Early Documents of the Dominican Sisters*. Vol. I Summit, N.J.: Dominican Nuns of Summit, 1969:7-22.

_____. "Letter of Humbert of the Romans Imposing the Constitutions (1259)." *Early Documents of the Dominican Sisters*. Vol. II Summit, N.J.: Dominican Nuns of Summit, 1969: 1-2.

Bernard of Clairvaux, *On the Song of Songs* I-IV. trans. Killian Walsh and Irene Edmonds. Spencer, Mass.: Cisterican Publications, 1971, 1979, 1980, 1983.

Boulding, Maria, trans. *The Confessions*. Hyde Park, NY: New York City Press, 2004.

Denifle, Henri."Über die Anfänge der Predigtweise der deutschen Mystiker." *Archiv für Literatur und Kirchengeschichte des Mittelalters*. Berlin: 1886, II

Ebner, Christina. *Offenbarungen*. Nürnberg Stadtbiblothek: MS Cent.V. App. 99.

Galvani, Christiane, trans. and Clark, Susan, ed. *Mechthild von Magdeburg: Flowing Light of the Divinity*. New York and London: Garland Publishing, Inc., 1991.

Grabmann, Martin. "Deutsche Mystik im Kloster Engelthal." *Sammelblatt des Historischen Vereins Eichstätt* 25/26, 1912.

Greith, Karl Johann. *Die Deutsche Mystik in Predigerordern von 1250-1350 nach ihren Grundlehren, Liedern und Lebensbildern aus Handschriflichen Quellen*. Freiburg: Herder, 1861; reprint Amsterdam: Ed. Rodopi, 1965.

Grundmann, Herbert. "Geschichtliche Grundlagen der deutschen Mystik" in Ruh, Kurt, ed. *Altdeutsche und Altniederdeutsche Mystik*: 82ff.

Haas, Alois. Preface to *Johannes Tauler* by Maria Shrady. New York and Mahwah; Paulist Press, 1985.

Hamburger, Jeffrey F. *The Rothschild Chronicles: Art and Mysticism in Flanders and the Rhineland around 1300*. New Haven and London: Yale University Press, 1990.

Haupt. Josef. ed. *Das Hohelied übersetzt von Williram, erklärt von Rilindis und Herrat, Äbtissinen zu Hohenburg in Elsass (1147-1196)*. Wien: Wilhelm Baumüller, 1864.

Hindsley, Leonard P. *Margaret Ebner: Major Works*. New York: Paulist Press, 1993.

Hoffmann, H. *Willirams Übersetzung und Auslegung des Hohenliedes in doppelten Texten aus den Breslauer und Leidener Handschriften herausgegeben und mit einem vollständigen Wörterbuche versehen*. Breslau: 1827

Heller, Nicholas. *The Exemplar: Life and Writings of Blessed Henry Suso, O.P.* Dubuque, Iowa: The Priory Press, 1962.

Krebs, Engelbert. "Die Mystik in Adelhausen: Eine vergleichende Studie über die Chronik der Anna von Munzingen und die Thaumatographische Literatur des 13. und 14. Jahrhunderts als Beitrag zur Geschichte der Mystik im Predigerorden". In: *Festgabe Heinrich Finke* (Münster i. W.: Druck und Verlag der Aschendorfischen Buchhandlung, 1904).

Langer, Otto. "Zur Dominikanischen Frauenmystik im spätmittelalterichen Deutschland." in Dinzelbacher, Peter, and

Bauer, Dieter K., eds. *Frauenmystik im Mittelalter.* Ostfildern bei Stuttgart: Schwabenverlag, 1985:341-346.

Lochner, Georg Wolfgang Karl. *Leben und Gesichte der Christine Ebnerin, Klosterfrau zu Engelthal.* Nürnberg, 1875.

Martini, Johann Christoph. *Historisch-geographische Beschreibung des ehemaligen berühmten Frauenklosters Engelthal.* Nürnberg, 1798.

Matter, E. Ann. *The Voice of My Beloved: The Song of Songs in Western Medieval Christianity.* Philadelphia: University of Pennsylvania Press, 1990.

Morel. P. Gall. *Offenbarungen der Schwester Mechthild von Magdeburg oder das fliessende Licht der Gottheit.* Darmstadt: Wissenschaftliche Buchgesellschaft, 1963.

Morgan, B.Q. and Strothman, F.W. eds. *Middle High German Translation of the Summa Theologica by Thomas Aquinas.* New York: 1967, 1st ed. 1950.

Oehl, Wilhelm. *Deutsche Mystikerbriefe des Mittelalters 1100-1550.* München: Georg Müller Verlag, 1931.

Oehl, Wilhelm. *Mechthild von Magdeburg: Das fliessende Licht der Gottheit* (=Sammlung Kösel 28, Deutsche Mystiker 2) Kempten/München: Artemis Verlag, 1911.

Ohly, Friedrich. ed., with Nicola Kleine. *Das St. Trutperter Hohelied: eine Lehre der liebenden Gotteserkenntnis.* Frankfurt am Main: Deutscher Klassiker Verlag, 1998.

Ohly, Friedrich. "Geist und Formen der Hoheliedauslegung im 12. Jahrhundert." *Zeitschrift für Deutsches Altertum* 85 (1954):181-197.

Pfeiffer, F. *Die Mystiker des 14. Jhrs.* Göttingen: Vandenhoeck & Ruprecht, 1907, 2 Bände.

Pope, Marvin. *The Song of Songs: A New Translation with Introduction and Commentary—The Anchor Bible.* Garden City, N.Y.: Doubleday and Company, 1977.

Preger, Wilhelm. *Geschichte der deutschen Mystik im Mittelalter.* Leipzig: Dorfling, 1881. 3 vol.

Reinitzer, Heimo. *Deutsche Bibelübersetzungen des Mittelalters.* Bern: Peter Lang Verlag, 1987/88.

Ringler, Siegfried. *Die Deutsche Literatur des Mittelaters Verfasserlexikon.* Berlin: Walter de Gruyter, 1985, V. s.v. "Langmann, Adelheid."

Ringler, Siegfried. *Viten- und Offenbarungsliteratur in Frauenklöstern des Mittelalters* München: Artemis Verlag, 1980.

Ruf, Paul, ed. *Mittelalterliche Bibliothekskataloge—Deutschlands und der Schweiz.* München: C.H. Beck'sche Verlag, MCMXXXII.

Ruh, Kurt, ed. *Altdeutsche und Altniederdeutsche Mystik* (Wege der Forschung XXIII); Darmstadt, 1964.

Ruh, Kurt. *Altdeutsche Mystik.* Bern: Francke Verlag, 1950.

Ruh, Kurt. *Medium Aevum* Band I, Aidos Verlag 1963.

Scheeben, Heribert Christian. "Über die Predigtweise der deutschen Mystiker" in Ruh, Kurt, ed. *Altdeutsche und Altniederdeutsche Mystik.* 101f.

Schmidt, Margot. *Mechthild von Magdeburg: Das Fliessende Licht der Gottheit.* Stuttgart-Bad Canstatt: Frommann-Holzboog Verlag, 1995.

Schröder, Karl, ed. *Der Nonne von Engelthal Büchlein von der Genaden Überlast.* Tübingen: H. Laupp, 1871.

Seemüller, Joseph. *Willirams deutsche Paraphrase des Hohenliedes mit Einleitung und Glossar.* Strassburg: Karl J. Trübner, 1878.

Shrady, Maria, trans. *Johannes Tauler: Sermons.* New York: Paulist Press, 1985.

Strauch, Philipp. *Die Offenbarungen der Adelheid Langmann, Klosterfrau zu Engelthal.* Strassburg: Karl J. Trübner, 1878.

Strauch, Philipp. *Margaretha Ebner und Heinrich von Nördlingen.* Freiburg i. B. and Tübingen: Akademische Verlagsbuchhandlung von J.C.B. Mohr, 1882; reprint Amsterdam: Verlag P. Schippers, N.V., 1966.

Tugwell, Simon. *Early Dominicnas: Selected Writings.* New York, Paulist Press, 1982.

Vicaire, M.-H. and Kathleen Pond, trans. *Saint Dominic and his Times.* New York: McGraw-Hill Book Company, 1964.

Voit, Gustav. *Engelthal: Geschichte eines Dominikanerinnenklösters im Nürnberger Raum.* Nürnberg: Verlag Korn und Bern, 1977.

Voit, Gustav. "Geschichte des Klosters Engelthal" in *750 Jahre Engelthal*. Simmelsdorf: Altnürnberger Landschaft e.V., 1994.

Walter, Wilhelm. *Die deutsche Bibelübersetzungen des Mittelalters* (188) Sp. 347.

Weinhandl, Margarethe. *Deutsches Nonnenleben: Das Leben der Schwestern zu Töss und der Nonne von Engelthal Büchlein von der Gnaden Überlast* in **Katholikon Werke und Urkunden**. II. München: O.C. Recht Verlag, 1921.

Wentzlaff-Eggebert, Friedrich Wilhelm. *Deutsche Mystik zwischen Mittelalter und Neuzeit,* Berlin: de Gruyter, 1969.

Wilms, Hieronymus. *Das älteste Verzeichnis der deutschen Dominikanerinnenklöster* in **Quellen und Forschungen zur Geschichte des Dominikanerordens in Deutschland** Leipzig: Otto Harrassowitz, 1928.

Wilms, Hieronymus. *Geschichte der deutschen Dominkanerinnen 1206-1916*. Dülmen i.W.: A. Laumann'sche Buchhandlung, 1920.

Author Biography

Leonard P. Hindsley, professor emeritus of German at Providence College authored three previous scholarly books on German mystics: *Margaret Ebner: Major Works* (Paulist Press) and *The Mystics of Engelthal: Writings from a Medieval Monastery* (St. Martin's Press) and *The Sister-Book of Engelthal* (Luminare Press). During thirty years teaching at Providence College Fr. Hindsley conducted courses in all levels of German language and literature. He also taught courses in Theology and in The Development of Western Civilization Program. He plans on publishing a book on St. Dominic's Nine Modes of Praying and a translation and commentary on the *Revelations* written by Dominican nun and mystic Christina Ebner (1277–1356).

Endnotes

1. Siegfried Ringler, *Die Deutsche Literatur des Mittelalters Verfasserlexikon* (Berlin and New York: Walter de Gruyter, 1985), Band 5, sp. 601. s.v. Langmann, Adelheid.

2. Gustav Voit, *Engelthal: Geschichte eines Dominikanerinnenklösters im Nürnberger Raum* (Nürnberg: Verlag Korn und Bern, 1977), 192.

3. Ibid., 192.

4. Philipp Strauch, *Die Offenbarungen der Adelheid Langmann, Klosterfrau zu Engelthal* (Straßburg: Karl J. Trübner, 1878), xvi; henceforth AL xvi

5. Voit, *Engelthal*, 194.

6. Strauch, AL xvi.

7. *Geschlecht-buch der stadt Nürnberg,* British Museum Library. German manuscript 10,009, 1559, s.v. Langmann,

8. Strauch, AL, xvi.

9. Ibid.

10. Voit, *Engelthal*, 192.

11. Johann Christoph Martini, *Historisch-geographische Beschreibung des ehemaligen berühmten Frauenklosters Engelthal* (Nürnberg/Altdorf. 1762; 2. Aufl. 1798), 80, 86.

12. Ibid., 114.

13. Voit, *Engelthal*, 193.

14. Voit, *Engelthal*, 25; Karl Schröder, ed., *Der Nonne von Engelthal Büchlein von der Gnaden Überlast* (Tübingen: H. Laupp, 1871) 7.

15. Voit, *Engelthal*, 25.

16. Leonard P. Hindsley, *The Sister-Book of Engelthal* (Eugene, OR: Luminare Press, 2023), 43.

17. Voit, *Engelthal*, 23.

18. Hindsley, *Sister-Book*, 44.

19. Ibid., 48.

20. Voit, *Engelthal*, 24.

21. Gustav Voit, "Geschichte des Klosters," *750 Jahre Engelthal* (Simmelsdorf: Altnürnberger Landschaft e.V., 1994), 11.

22. Voit, *Engelthal*, 25, fn 69.

23. Hindsley, *Sister-Book*, 45.

24. Schröder, *Der Nonne*, 7; Voit, *Engelthal*, 25.

25. Voit, *Engelthal*, 25.

26. Ibid.

27. Ibid., 26.

28. Schröder, *Der Nonne*, 7; Voit, *Engelthal*, 27 (my translation).

29. Voit, *Engelthal*, 27.

30. Ibid.

31. Ibid., 207-209.

32. Strauch, AL, 73.

33. Voit, *Engelthal*, 35.

34. Voit, "Geschichte des Klosters," 16.

35. Ibid., 16-17.

36. Ibid., 44. Charles IV (1315-1378) became king of Bohemia in 1346 and assumed the imperial dignity in 1355.

37. Voit, *Engelthal*, 44; G.W.K Lochner, *Leben und Geschichte der Christina Ebnerin, Klosterfrau zu Engelthal* (Nürnberg: August Recknagel's Buchhandlung, 1872), 25, (my translation).

38. Voit, *Engelthal*, 44; Lochner, *Leben*, 26.

39. Voit, *Engelthal*, 44; Lochner, *Leben*, 27f, 35f.

40. Voit, *Engelthal*, 40.

41. Ibid., 41.

42. Voit, "Geschichte des Klosters," 20.

43. Hieronymus Wilms, *Das Älteste Verzeichnis der deutschen Dominikanerinnenklöster* in *Quellen und Forschungen zur Geschichte*

des Dominikanerordens in Deutschland (Leipzig: Otto Harrassowitz, 1928), 71.

44. Marie-Humbert Vicaire, *St. Dominic and His Times,* translated by Kathleen Pond (New York: McGraw Hill, 1964), 122.

45. "The Primitive Constitutions of the Monastery of San Sisto," *Early Documents of the Dominican Sisters,* Vol. I. (Summit, N.J.: Dominican Nuns of Summit, 1969), 7.

46. *Early Documents,* I, 7.

47. Ibid., II, 1-2.

48. Ibid., II, 2.

49. Ibid., II, 5.

50. Hindsley, *Sister-Book,* 76.

51. Ibid., 61,

52. Strauch, *Adelheid Langmann,* 68:11. Henceforth, this will be cited as *Adelheid Langmann,* but when I refer to the manuscript transcription, it will appear as AL.

53. Margarethe Weinhandl, *Deutsches Nonnenleben: Das Leben der Schwestern zu Töß und der Nonne von Engelthal Büchlein von der Gnaden Überlast* in *Katholikon Werke und Urkunden,* II (München: O.C. Recht Verlag, 1921), 29.

54. Ibid., 18-19,

55. *Early Documents,* II, 33.

56. Weinhandl, *Deutsches Nonnenleben,* 21.

57. *Early Documents,* II, 37.

58. Ibid., 38.

59. *Early Documents,* II, 12.

60. Weinhandl, *Deutsches Nonnenleben,* 36.

61. *Early Documents,* II, 14-15.

62. Ibid., II, 16-17.

63. Ibid., 17,

64. Simon Tugwell, O.P., *Early Dominicans: Selected Writings* (New York: Paulist Press, 1982), 70.

65. *Early Documents,* II, 33.

66. Ibid., 34,

67. Ibid., 7.

68. Ibid., 22-23.

69. Cod. Cent. VIII, 79, Nürnberg, Stadtbibliothek.

70. Ibid., 25. 1-48.

71. Paul Ruf, ed., *Mittelalterliche Bibliothekskataloge—Deutschlands und der Schweiz* 3,1 1932, (München: Beck'sche Verlag, 1932), 645.

72. Martin Grabmann, "Deutsche Mystik in Kloster Engelthal," *Sammelblatt des historischen Vereins Eichstätt* 25/26, (1912), 33-44.

73. Weinhandl, *Deutsches Nonnenleben*, 17.

74. Hieronymus Wilms, *Geschichte der deutschen Dominikanerinnen (1206-1916)*, Dülmen i.W.: Laumann'sche Buchhandlung, 1920, 75-76.

75. Weinhandl, *Deutsches Nonnenleben*, 35.

76. Grabmann, "Deutsche Mystik," 34.

77. Margot Schmidt in Hindsley, *Margaret Ebner*, 46-47.

78. CEN, LXXr (my translation).

79. CEN, XVIv (my translation).

80. Wilhelm Preger, *Geschichte der deutschen Mystik im Mittelalter* (Leipzig: Dorfling & Franke, 1881, 3 vols., Reprint Basel: Otto Zeller Verlagsbuchhandlung, 1962), 275-276; AL 122b; Strauch, 37:14f.

81. Siegfried Ringler, ed., *Die deutsche Literatur des Mittelalters Verfasserlexikon* (Berlin: Walter de Gruyter, 1985), 602; Strauch, *Adelheid Langmann*, 61:12-66:7.

82. Henri Denifle, "Über die Anfänge der Predigtweise der deutschen Mystiker," *Archiv für Literatur und Kirchengeschichte des Mittelalters* (Berlin/Freiburg: B. Herder, 1886), 645.

83. Tugwell, *Early Dominicans*, 327-329.

84. Wilms, *Dominikanerinnen*, 72.

85. Ibid., 73.

86. Otto Langer, "Zur dominikanischen Frauenmystik im spätmittelalterlichen Deutschland," in Peter Dinzelbacher and Dieter K. Bauer, eds. *Frauenmystik im Mittelalter* (Ostfildern bei Stuttgart: Schwabenverlag, 1985), 342-343.

87. Weinhndl, *Deutsches Nonnenleben*, 33.

88. Langer, "Frauenmystik," 342-343.

89. Ibid., 346.

90. Philipp Strauch, *Margaretha Ebner und Heinrich von Nötdlingen* (Freiburg i. B. and Tübingen: Akademische Verlagsbuchhandlung von J. C. B Mohr, 1882), reprint Amsterdam: Verlag P. Schippers, N.V., 1966), 270-271.

91. Alois Haas in Preface to Josef Schmidt, ed, and Maria Shrady, trans., *Johannes Tauler: Sermons* (New York: Paulist Press, 1985), xii.

92. Ibid., xiii.

93. Ibid., xxiv.

94. Joseph Schmidt, *Johannes Tauler*, 164.

95. Ibid., 165.

96. Nicholas Heller, *The Exemplar; Life and Writings of Blessed Henry Suso, O.P.* (Dubuque, IA: The Priory Press, 1962), II, 117-127.

97. Ibid., , II, 335.

98. Weinhandl, *Deutsches Nonnenleben*, 36-37.

99. Ibid., 37-38, quoting Engelbert Krebs, "Die Mystik in Adelhausen" Eine vergleichende Studie über die Chronik der Anna von Munzingen und die Thaumotographische Literatur des 13. und 14. Jahrhunderts als Beitrag zur Geschichte der Mystik im Predigerorden," *Festgabe Heinrich Finke* (Münster: Aschendorff, 1904), 87.

100. Codex *2686*, Wien, Nationalbibliothek.

101. Paul Ruf, ed., *Mittelalterliche Bibliothekskataloge*, 638-650. This refers to the fact that these texts were read on specific feasts or in specific seasons.

102. Friedrich Ohly, ed., *Das St. Trutperter Hohelied: eine Lehre der liebenden Gotteserkenntnis* (Frankfurt am Main: Deutscher Klassikerverlag, 1998), 327.

103. Ibid., 34; line 28f.: "vone diu sô newart nie nehein | sêle sô lieplîche geküsset. Der munt dâ mite | si kuste, daz was ir wille unde ir minne... der | munt ist zuogetân küssende, er wirt ûfgetân | sprechende. er hete si è geküsset è er ir zuo | spreche. Er was der küssende, sie minnende. | si was diu gekuste, in minnende."

104. Ibid., 38.

105. Ibid.

106. AL 134a: "ich wil nit gewandelt werden in dich, sunder du solt gewandelt werden in mich."

107. Ohly, *Hohelied*, 154. "niht daz ich in dich verwandelet werde alsô | das essen des lîbes, sunder dû solt in mich verwandelet werde."

108. Ibid. The quotes are based on a passage from Saint Augustine's *Confessions* (Book VII:16) ". . . and I seemed to hear your voice from on high: 'I am the food of the mature; grow then, and you will eat me. You will not change me into yourself like bodily food: you will be changed into me." Maria Boulding, trans., *The Confessions* (Hyde Park: New York City Press, 2004) 173.

109. Josef Haupt, ed., *Das Hohelied übersetzt von Willliram, erklärt von Rilindis und Herrat, Äbtissinnen zu Hohenburg in Elsass (1147-1196)*, (Wien: Wilhelm Baumüller, 1864), 66.

110. Ibid., 136. A *kemenate* was a heated room in a monastery where the nuns could warm themselves in winter. In the context I have usually translated it as a Lady's chamber and here it would be Christ's chamber. It stands for a comfortable room in which the lovers could meet privately in secret.

111. Bernard of Clairvaux, *On the Song of Songs*. Trans. Killian Walsh and Irene Edmonds (Spencer, MA: Cistercian Publications, 1971-83), I, 6:9.

112. Ibid., I, 7:2.

113. Ibid., II, 27:1.

114. Ibid., II, 27:1.

115. Ibid., II, 23:3.

116. Ibid., II, 23:16.

117. Ibid., I, 9:2.

118. Ibid., I, 3:2.

119. Ibid., I, 4:2.

120. Ibid., I, 4:1.

121. Ibid., I, 2:9.

122. Ibid., I, 8:7b-8.

123. Ibid., I, 8:2.

124. Ibid., II, 38:5.

125. Ibid.

126. Ibid., IV, 67:1.

127. Ibid., II, 27:8.

128. Ibid.

129. Ibid., IV, 71:10.

130. Ibid., IV, 71:8.

131. Weinhandl, *Deutsches Nonnenleben*, 14.

132. Margot Schmidt in Hindsley, *Margaret Ebner*, 33.

133. Strauch, *Margaretha Ebner*, 246:17f. Letter XIII (my translation).

134. Ibid., 248-249; *156-159.

135. Ibid., 247.

136. Ibid., 210.

137. Ibid., 266.

138. Ringler, *Verfasserlexikon*, col. 298.

139. Strauch, *Adelheid Langmann*, 100.

140. Gail Morel, *Offenbarungen der Schwester Mechthild von Magdeburg oder das fliessende Licht der Gottheit* (Darmstadt: Wissenschaftliche Buchgesellschaft, 1963), 33; M. Schmidt, *Das fließende Licht der Gottheit* (Stuttgat-Bad Cannstatt: Frommann-Holzboog Verlag, 1995) 47. All translations are mine.

141. Morel, *Offenbarungen*, 40; Schmidt, *Das fließende Licht*, 56.

142. Weinhandl, *Deutsches Nonnenleben*, 41; AL, 91.

143. Frank Tobin, *Mechthild of Magdeburg: The Flowing Light of the Godhead* (New York and Mahwah: Paulist Press, 1998), 235.

144. Morel, *Offenbarungen*, 66; Schmidt, *Das fließende Licht*, 89.

145. Morel, *Offenbarungen*, 85; Schmidt, *Das fließende Licht*, 11; Galvani, *Mechthild*, 89.

146. Morel, *Offenbarungen*, 56; Schmidt, *Das fließende Licht*, 77.

147. Schmidt, *Das fließende Licht*, 78.

148. Ibid.

149. Morel, *Offenbarungen*, 11, 64; Schmidt, *Das fließende Licht*, 20, 86; Galvani, *Mechthild*, 14, 68.

150. Morel, *Offenbarungen*, 8, 28, 33, 41; Schmidt, *Das fließende Licht*, 15, 43, 47, 57; Galvani, *Mechthild*, 12, 31, 36, 44.

151. Wilhelm Oehl, *Deutsche Mystikerbriefe des Mittelalters 1100-1550* (München: Georg Müller Verlag, 1931), 393.

152. Strauch, *Adelheid Langmann*, xx.

153. Ringler, *Viten*, 19-28.

154. Ibid., 73.

155. Ibid., 74.

156. Wilhelm Oehl, *Mysteriker*, 394-396; for Letter 1 see AL, 311v-212v; for Letter 2 see AL., 312v-214r; for Letter 3 see AL., 214r-211v; for the rest of the text of the letters see AL., 209r-211v.

157. Strauch, *Margaretha Ebner*, Letter LIX, 272:10-11.

158. The manuscript begins in Latin: "In nomine Patris et Filii et Spiritus Sancti" and continues in Middle High German, as if the autobiographical text were a prayer or even a sermon. Manuscript B (Berlin) contains the following introduction to the text on page 86v: "In the year of Our Lord 1300 or more in the city of Nuremberg there was a venerable family named Langmann, related to the Ebner family. From that family was born a child named Adelheid. What wonders God performed with her from the time of her childhood and what the Holy Spirit worked with her, you will presently hear. Whatever was seemly, praiseworthy, spiritual or godly the child possessed without being boisterous" (my translation).

159. The Langmann family worshiped at the parish Church of St. Sebaldus in Nuremberg. Their coat-of-arms appears in that church in a stained glass window located in the apse. The heraldic shield of the Ebners appears in the same window.

160. The term "martyrdom" refers to Christ's passion and death on the cross. He is the prime martyr for whom all subsequent Christian martyrs suffer and die.

161. Secondary sources such as the *Lexikon der Frau* often assume that Adelheid was married and widowed. Her own text does not support this unambiguously although later (5) she refers to herself as a widow. Gustav Voit gives the name of her husband as Gottfried Teufel.

162. The feast of the two apostles was celebrated on May 1.

163. The discipline refers to self-flagellation. It was understood by

Dominicans to be a means of self-discipline to fight against temptation and to grow in virtue as exemplified by Saint Dominic's Third Mode of Praying.

164. These were instruments used for executions. See Strauch, fn to 4:20.

165. The devil disguised himself as her "muhme." This word could be translated as "aunt," "cousin," or any female relative.

166. Adelheid refers to herself as "the nun." The *Veni Creator Spiritus* is a sequence sung at monastic profession ceremonies to invoke the sending of the Holy Spirit upon the professing sister that she may live by the Spirit of the Lord.

167. The exact number of virgins mentioned links them to Saint Ursula and her eleven-thousand companions, devotion to whom was popular throughout the Middle Ages in Germany and elsewhere.

168. Normally when a novice was admitted she would be clothed with the habit by the superior or some other designated person.

169. Trinity Sunday was the first Sunday after Pentecost.

170. The original text reads "*pei dir.*" This can be interpreted to mean "within you." This accords with the Pauline teaching on the indwelling of the Spirit. It is also reminiscent of Tauler's doctrine of the birth in the soul of the believer.

171. The entire passage beginning with "Peace be with you" and ending with the same is very like the post-resurrection appearances of Jesus to his disciples recorded in the Gospels. In that vein Dr. Josef Pestel in his translation of the *Revelations* published in 1939, interpreted the conclusion of this paragraph as "he disappeared."

172. The Assumption of the Blessed Virgin Mary is celebrated on August 15th. When the phrase "she received Our Lord" is used, it refers to reception of Holy Communion.

173. This section of the translation follows the arrangement of manuscript M which logically places the account of events around Adelheid's profession of vows together. Manuscript B and Strauch's edition places this passage after paragraph 87. Prestel likewise places it in this position.

174. A shawm is a double-reed wind instrument related to the oboe.

175. The word used here is *ostergloien,* daffodils.

176. The "book of life" refers to the biblical Book of Revelation (3:5):

"He who conquers shall be clad thus in white garments, and I will not blot his name out of the book of life; I will confess his name before my Father and his angels." See also Revelation (13:8; 17:8; 22:12). "And I saw the dead, great and small, standing before the throne, and books were opened. And the dead were judged by what they had done." Revelation 12:15; Exod. 12:32; Ps. 69:28; Dan. 12:1; 3:5; Mal. 3:16; Luke 10:20.

177. Rev. 3:19: "Those whom I love I reprove and chasten; so be zealous and repent."

178. 28 December is the feast of the Holy Innocents.

179. The Epiphany or Three Kings' Day is 6 January.

180. The eve of Candlemas or Presentation of the Lord is 1 February.

181. Candlemas is 2 February.

182. Paragraph (67) appears in numerical sequence in manuscript B. In manuscript M it follows paragraph (22) where it may have been placed by a later redactor because it seems to fit there logically from the context. The same paragraph (67) will also appear after paragraph 66 as in manuscript B.

183. In the Middle Ages the Virgin Mary was often portrayed artistically with her mantle wrapped protectively around groups of people. Saint Dominic himself dreamt that all the Dominicans were huddled under her mantle.

184. Paragraph (23) does not appear in manuscript M.

185. As Strauch points out this is the first definite date in the *Revelations*. If the dates follow from this point on then the visions up to paragraph (71) would cover the years 1330-1336.

186. It was common belief that the taking of religious vows restored the nun to baptismal innocence, as if no sins had ever been committed prior to the profession of vows.

187. The inscription of the name on the heart of Christ and on Adelheid's heart is reminiscent of the incident in which Henry Suso asked to have the name of Jesus written upon his heart. See Nicholas Heller. *The Exemplar: Life and Writings of Blessed Henry Suso, O.P.*, trans, Sr, M. Ann Edward, O.P. (Dubuque: The Priory Press, 1962), p. 13: After having inscribed IHS on his chest with a stylus Suso exclaimed, "Oh Lord, my sole delight, behold how eagerly my heart craves to be united

with thee. I myself cannot imprint thee more deeply on my heart, but I beg thee to complete the work and carve thy sacred name deep down into my inmost soul, so that we will never be separated." This writing of the name also appears in Rev. 3:12.

188. Christ is portrayed as coming to judge the living and the dead on the Last Day. This image, while widely popular in the Middle Ages, also derives from the Book of Revelation (Rev. 1:16; 2:12 etc.) which Adelheid used consciously as a scriptural source for her own *Revelations*.

189. Holy Trinity was celebrated on the first Sunday after Pentecost 1330.

190. Manuscript B has "Johanns Evangelisten" which would place this feast on December 27. From the context it seems more likely that Adelheid refers to the Nativity of John the Baptist (June 24). However, Voit (p. 243) maintains that this feast was kept at Engelthal on the Tuesday after Easter which would also fit the context.

191. 31 March 1331.

192. 28 April 1331: St. Peter the Preacher is also known as St. Peter Martyr, the proto-martyr of the Dominican Order. His feast was kept on April 29.

193. The nine choirs of angels are Seraphim, Cherubim, Thrones, Dominations (Dominions), Virtues, Powers, Principalities, Archangels and Angels.

194. 29 April 1331.

195. The inscription of the Name of Jesus on her heart recalls again the experience of Henry Suso and may also be linked to Rev. 3:12: "He who conquers, I will make him a pillar in the temple of my God; never shall he go out of it, and I will write on him the name of my God . . . : It may also link Adelheid with Margaret Ebner (1291-1351) with whom Christ exchanged hearts. With Adelheid, the inscription is exchanged. In both cases, the action unites Christ and the mystic nun so that she may proclaim with Saint Paul: "It is no longer I who live, but Christ lives in me (Gal. 2:20)."

196. The feast of the translation of Saint Dominic was celebrated on 23 May 1331.

197. This passage is a paraphrase from the Song of Songs (Cant. 4:11): "Your lips distil nectar, my bride; honey and milk are under your tongue; the scent of your garments is like the scent of Lebanon." The summer solstice occurred on 24 June 1332.

198. The passage in brackets also appears in the Stuttgart manuscript of Christina Ebner's *Revelations*, p. 27a. The revelation concerns two other sisters of Engelthal. Of Sister Erlint nothing is known. She is not mentioned again by Adelheid Langmann nor is she included among the brief biographical sketches written by Christina Ebner in the *Sister-Book* of Engelthal. From documentary evidence cited by Voit there is no mention of a nun named Erlint at the Monastery of Engelthal.

199. The feast of Saint Mary Magdalene was celebrated on 22 July 1332. It was a semiduplex feast since she was an original patroness of the Dominican Order.

200. Lists of nuns in a Dominican monastery often identify each sister by her place in choir. The nuns and friars took their places in chapel according to the "order of religion" which was determined by office and then by date of entry into the monastery.

201. By leaning against the breast of Christ, Adelheid imitates Saint John the Beloved at the Last Supper (John 13:23-25). Like him, she has been called "Beloved" and like him she will receive secret knowledge of Christ through revelations.

202. The Assumption was celebrated on 15 August 1332.

203. The feast of the Dedication of the Church depended on the dedication day of the local church. Gustav Voit does not list a specific day for this celebration at Engelthal although Christina Ebner also mentions the same feast several times in her own *Revelations* where it seems to have been celebrated on the Sunday after the Assumption of the Blessed Virgin Mary (Nürnberg manuscript Xa). Voit shows that on the Fifth Sunday after Easter the nuns processed with the pastor and father confessor through the cloister walk to commemorate the dedication of the church (244). The dedication of the new chapel was held on Saint Egidius Day, 1 September (247).

204. This preacher is called a *lesmeister* in the text. According to A. Haas a *lesmeister* was an academic responsible for the education of novices, whereas a *lebmeister* served as spiritual director of the novices. See Josef Schmidt's introduction to *Johannes Tauler: Sermons* (Paulist Press, N.Y.), 1985, p. 3.

205. The identity of this man is unknown. Since Adelheid Langmann notes that he is a Dominican, he could not be Henry of Nördlingen, who

had asked Margaret Ebner to write down her *Revelations*. He may be Konrad of Füssen, who was the spiritual director of Christina Ebner. He must have been known to Adelheid Langmann.

206. Cant. 4:11: "Your lips distil nextar, my bride, honey and milk are under your tongue; the scent of your garments is like the scent of Lebanon."

207. Cant. 4:7: "You are all fair, my love, there is no flaw in you."

208. Adelheid alludes to the Song of Songs (Cant. 1:2): "O that you would kiss me with the kisses of your mouth!" She may also be influenced by Saint Bernard of Clairvaux's *On the Song of Songs*.

209. Cant. 4:7.

210. The image of Saint John resting upon the breast of Christ formed a part of popular medieval iconography. Margaret Ebner also experienced an incident similar to the one described here. See Hindsley, *Margaret Ebner: Major Works*, (Paulist Press, N.Y., 1993), p. 118.

211. The wounds of Christ were also called *"minnewerke"*—the works of love, which connected them to the motive for Christ's suffering and death — love for the Father and love for the whole human race.

212. Adelheid Langmann had several relatives who were also nuns at Engelthal. This aunt may have been Gerhaus Meyer who shared the revenues from an estate at Traunfeld with Adelheid (Voit, p. 194).

213. The venia was both a gesture of adoration and an action of repentance. To make a venia the nun had to throw herself forward to the floor, landing on her right side while holding the scapular extended in her right hand. Dominicans typically used this prayer gesture immediately prior to receiving Holy Communion or to make amends for faults. Adelheid Langmann also used the venia as part of her private prayer, just as Saint Dominic had done.

214. The celebration of St. Ursula and the eleven-thousand virgins was 21 October 1332.

215. The previous section marked in brackets [] is the text from manuscript B. The text following it in parentheses is the alternative text from manuscript M that replaces the bracketed text from B.

216. Strauch (p. 102) believes there is a connection between this passage and *Das Hohe Lied* (ed. J. Haupt (66:10): "wahs unde iz mich; nicht daz ich in dich verwandolst wurde also daz essen des libes, sundir

diu solt in mich verwandelot werden." Both texts quote St. Augustine in his *Confessions* (VI.10.16).

217. Saint Stephen Day was 26 December 1332.

218. Three Kings Day is also called Epiphany and was celebrated 6 January.

219. Her soul is reading the great hymn of praise to the Most Holy Trinity. This indicates the presence of her soul before the Triune God while in a state of ecstasy.

220. In AL *weissen suntag.* Prestel interprets that to be *Invocavit* Sunday, that is, the first Sunday in Lent.

221. In AL there is a brief lacuna in the text, but not in M. *Te Deum Patrem ungenitum, te Filium ingenitum, te Spiritum Sanctum paraclitum, sanctam et individuum Trinitatem, toto corde et ore confitemur, laudamus atque benedicimus: tibi gloria in saecula* was the antiphon to the Magnificat for the second vespers of the feast of the Most Holy Trinity. *Beati immaculati* is the beginning of Psalm 118 (119:1-8). This psalm was recited over the hours of prime, terce, sext and none each day. *Requiem aeternum dona eis, Domine et lux perpetua luceat eis* is the introit to the Mass for the Dead. The *Miserere* is Psalm 56 (57).

222. The vigil of the Chair of Saint Peter was 21 February 1333.

223. *Benedictio Dei omnipotentis Patris et Filii et Spiritus Sancti descendat super vos (te) et meneat semper.*

224. 24 February.

225. The vigil of Saint John the Evangelist was 26 December 1333.

226. 27 December 1333.

227. 25 March 1334.

228. Jeffrey Hamburger writes of this image as a commonplace in German mysticism. Adelheid Langmann may have been influenced by the mystical poem *Granum sinapsis*. An early fourteenth-century commentary on this poem states: "de mystico deserto, quod est divinum ipsum." See Jeffrey Hamburger, *The Rothschild Chronicles: Art and Mysticism in Flanders and the Rhineland circa 1300* (New Haven and London: Yale University Press, 1990), pp. 54-55.

229. *Deus, Deus meus respice* is Psalm 21 (22). That is the psalm verse quoted by Christ on the cross: "My God, my God, why hast thou

forsaken me?" This fits the context. The antiphon *Christus factus obediens* is used liturgically during the Paschal Triduum, during the services on Good Friday and Holy Saturday. The antiphon is based on Phil. 2:8: "And being found in human form he humbled himself and became obedient unto death—even death on a cross."

230. This prayer is rhymed in the Middle High German.

231. Adelheid Langmann's reticence about her miracles reminds one of Christ's admonition to remain silent about his deeds (Matt. 8:4; 9:30; 12:16).

232. The Assumption was on 15 August 1334.

233. Christina of Kornburg is mentioned in the *Sister-Book* of Engelthal. In a lengthy passage she is described as being especially faithful to choral prayer, to learning and to keeping silence. Her final illness lasted for two years during which she suffered greatly, but nonetheless had great divine joy as if "drunk" on "Cyprian wine." Her final passion was revealed to others after her death. See Hindsley, *Sister-Book*, pp. 76-78.

234. This detail is both reminiscent of the post-resurrection appearances of Christ to the apostles, especially to the "doubting" Thomas, and also to the event of the Annunciation where the angel Gabriel appeared to Mary in her "cell."

235. According to documentary evidence Christina of Kornburg was alive in 1335, but probably died before 1340 since Christina Ebner includes Kornburg's biography among the deceased nuns of Engelthal. See Schröder, p. 30; Voit, p. 190.

236. The exetatrix was charged with the task of waking the other sisters.

237. This nun died before 1340 (Voit, p. 199). There were other nuns at Engelthal with the same surname—Adelheid, her daughters Adelheid and Jeut, and Elsbet. In the text the surnames of nuns sometimes use the feminine ending -in, as in Ortlibin which in modern German would be Ortlieb.

238. 17 July 1335; Aachen had a shrine to the Virgin Mary that was a popular place of pilgrimage in the Middle Ages.

239. Adelheid Langmann records various instruments used by her to administer the discipline. This act of self-flagellation imitated the scourging of Christ at the pillar and therefore helped the flagellant to participate

in the martyrdom of Christ. Taking the discipline was a common practice in the Middle Ages and the Dominican Constitutions included it as an obligatory practice for all members. "Discipline" appears as the third of Saint Dominic's Modes of Praying. There it functions as a prayer gesture used to symbolize the need for leading a disciplined Christian life as indicated by the text accompanying the gesture: "Disciplina tua correxit me in finem" (Your discipline has corrected me to the end.) The items mentioned by Adelheid show an increase in the severity of her practice.

240. In all the manuscripts Eberhard of Hohenstein is termed a *rihter*, but this would be more logically *ritter*. A knight could also conceivably serve as a judge. Hohenstein Castle still exists in the vicinity of Hersbruck not far from the village of Engelthal.

241. 31 December.

242. The Solemnity of Corpus Christ was celebrated on the Thursday after Trinity Sunday.

243. Kaisheim was a Cistercian monastery in the vicinity of the Dominican monastery of nuns at Maria Medingen near Dillingen on the Danube fouunded in 1135 and suppressed in 1803. Kaisheim had particularly good relations with the Dominican nuns of Maria Medingen. The prior, Ulrich III, wrote letters to the mystic of Medingen, Margaret Ebner, five of which are extant. The two monasteries also exchanged manuscripts for copying. It is likely that a close connection also existed between Kaisheim and Engelthal due perhaps to Henry of Nördlingen who was known and respected by the nuns of Maria Medingen and Engelthal.

244. 15 August.

245. The text in brackets [] appears only in Manuscript B. The following passage in parentheses () appears in Manuscript M and replaces the text in Manuscript B.

246. Dominican nuns built their churches with a large gallery above the nave, facing the sanctuary below. This gallery contained the nuns' choir and an altar. From the gallery the nuns could observe the celebration of the Mass at the main altar in the church without seeing or being seen by the people below.

247. The names of the virgins, *Spes* (Hope) and *Caritas* (Love) were always written in Latin whenever used in the document. Strauch notes

a possible influence of Lamprecht's *Tochter von Sion*, a brief version of which was also known to Christina Ebner (Strauch, p. 108).

248. The text from here to paragraph 80 appears in manuscript M, but not in manuscript B.

249. This nun was probably Elsbet Mayer. She was the "muhme" of Mechthild Langmann and died before 1340. Christina Ebner included her biographical sketch in the *Sister-Book* of Engelthal. See Hindsley, *Sister-Book*, 91.

250. This refers to the Solemnity of the Annunciation celebrated on 25 March. Easter fell on 27 March 1334.

251. Adelheid refers to herself here.

252. The language used in this passage is reminiscent of the Song of Songs (2:10) and the request to kiss the wounds of Christ shows the influence of the sermons On the Song of Songs by Saint Bernard of Clairvaux (61:3-4; 5-8; 62:7).

253. The interdict was imposed by Pope John XXII upon Emperor Louis IV (the Bavarian) who died 11 October 1342. Louis was a friend of the nuns of Engelthal, gave them gifts and received the sympathy and prayerful support of the nuns (Lochner, p. 21).

254. The people of various parts of the empire suffered from hunger, the flooding of the Rhine River and the Danube, earthquakes, severe winters and fire (Strauch, p. 109).

255. This Mass is also mentioned in Christina Ebner's *Sister-Book* (Hindsley, *Sister-Book*, p. 74). According to the Chronicles of Nuremberg (3, 328,25) he was a Dominican.

256. Geut was prioress 1340-1349. The conflict mentioned here may have been with the prominent Schenk of Reicheneck family which made claims over the real estate and revenues of the monastery. Strauch also mentions a dispute between clergy and civil authorites in Nuremberg (p. 110).

257. "You" is singular "du".

258. St. Louis Day is 25 August.

259. *Gaudeamus* is the introit for a virgin. The introit for Louis would have been *Os justi meditabitur*.

260. Paragraph 88 appears in this position in manuscript B, but has

already appeared in this translation in the position it has in manuscript M, in the middle of paragraph 14.

261. The feast of St. Thomas the Preacher refers to that of St. Thomas Aquinas which seems to have been celebrated on 21 December because he was a "Hawbtherr des Ordens." See Voit, p. 250.

262. All Saints is 1 November.

263. That souls, having been completely purged of sin and its effects, must still wait to see God is not Church teaching, but the opinion of ecstatic visionaries such as Christina Ebner (Stuttgart. 118b).

264. Jutta Pfinzing was the sister of Berthold Pfinzing the Elder and Elsbet, also a nun of Engelthal. She was sister-in-law of Christina Ebner, whose sister Jutta had married Berthold Pfinzing. Jutta may also have been prioress of Engelthal from 8 October 1340 to 15 August 1341. The Pfinzings were an important family of Nuremberg and are mentioned in the *Geschlecht-Buch der Stat Nürnberg* on page 8, where a coat-of-arms appears along with a description of the family of Conradt Pfinzing in 1318. Gustav Voit lists eleven Pfinzing women as nuns of Engelthal (pp. 200-203).

265. Pope Saint Mark is 7 October.

266. Manuscript M omits the section in brackets and replaces it with the phrase in parentheses.

267. All Saints in 1 November.

268. Saint Matthew Day was 24 February. This vision appears only in manuscript M.

269. Saint Mary of Egypt (d. 340), known also as Mary the Harlot was famous in legend for her ascetic life of penance.

270. Luke 1:26-28.

271. Luke 1:28; 31-34: "How can this be, since I have no husband?"

272. Luke 1:30, 35: "Do not be afraid, Mary, for you have found favor with God" and "The Holy Spirit will come upon you, and the power of the Most High will overshadow you."

273. Luke 1:38: "Behold, I am the handmaid of the Lord, let it be done to me according to your word."

274. Luke 1: 40-41.

275. Luke 2:7.

276. Luke 2:8-15.

277. Luke 2:22-24.

278. Matt. 2:1.

279. Matt. 2:2.

280. Matt. 2:11.

281. Luke 2:22, 24-28.

282. Luke 2:35.

283. Matt. 2:16.

284. Matt. 2:13-15.

285. Luke 2:45.

286. Luke 2:46.

287. Luke 2:48.

288. Matt. 3:13-16.

289. Matt. 3:17: "This is my beloved Son with whom I am well pleased." Adelheid quoted the scripture verse in Latin: "Hic est filius meus dilectus in quo mihi bene complacui."

290. Matt. 4:2.

291. Luke 4:2; Matt. 4:3f.

292. John 2:2-10.

293. "Cyprian wine" occurs in many mystical texts and is used in *Das Hohe Lied* (Haupt 25:1; 66:3), (Hindsley, Sister-Book, p. 77) and in Christina Ebner's *Offenbarungen* (p. 53)

294. Luke 7:36-38.

295. John 4:16-18.

296. John 8:3-7.

297. Matt. 21:2-9; John 12:14-15.

298. Matt. 26:47; Mark 14:43; Luke 22:47; John 18:2-5.

299. Matt. 26:15.

300. Matt. 26:20-35; Mark 14:18-31; Luke 22:13-38.

301. This friend is Ulrich III Niblung, abbot of Kaisheim 1340-1360. Five letters from him to Margaret Ebner are extant.

302. 21 September.

303. This letter from Ulrich, abbot of Kaisheim, is Letter 1 in Oehl, p. 394.

304. "Him" refers to the devil.

305. This letter is from Adelheid to Ulrich. Oehl lists it as Letter 2 (p. 395).

306. This letter is from Ulrich to Adelheid, Letter 3 in Oehl (p. 395).

Index to the Translated Texts

Numbers refer to paragraph numbers, not to page numbers

Aachen, Our Lady of   68
Absolution   53, 54
Adelheid Langmann
    at 13 years old   2
    aunt   46, 90
    "aunt" = devil   7
    Beloved   19, 27, 35, 36, 43, 51, 72
    beside herself   20
    bride   16, 19
    child, sister, bride   8
    entrance to Engelthal   85-86
    family   6
    flame   22, 24
    foreknowledge   47
    Love   41, 56, 62, 65, 76
    mother   91
    new baptism   56
Adelheid's responses
    "I want whatever your want"   32
    "It is the great love that I bear for you"   42
    "Heaven is nothing to me …"   42
    "O loving Lord …"   65
    "Go away, you evil spirit …"   71
    "I am yearning for him …"   72
    "By the living God I order you …"   92

Adelheid's responses (*cont.*)
    "Be gone ... I command you"   92
    "He looked upon me ..."   93
    "Receive all the cries amd voices as if they came from my own mouth"   94
    "Draw me to you with love ..."   144
    "He looked upon me with the eyes of his mercy and his eyes were filled with love"   159

Adultery, woman caught in   144
Advent   15, 50, 72
All Saints Day   91, 92
Altar   21, 26, 30, 48, 76
    of St. John   157
Agnus Dei   11, 19
Apostles   32, 52
Angels   14, 29, 32, 48, 52, 55, 64, 72, 81, 82, 83, 88, 95, 96, 99, 100, 105, 114
    choirs   29, 32, 55, 87
    Gabriel   32, 79, 155
Annunciation   52, 58, 79, 95-102; Day 80
Apostles   82
Assumption   13, 34, 63, 70, 82
Ave Maria   52, 68, 70, 79, 81

Baptism   25
Beati Dei Genetrix   82
Beati immaculati   52
Bed   21, 72, 75, 159
Benedictio Dei   53
Berchtold of Moosburg   84
Birth, spiritual   106
Blacksmith   113
Blessed Sacrament   82
Book of life=Christ's heart   15
Bow, profound   50

Breast, sucking   75
Bride   159
Bridegroom   95, 159

Cana, wedding at   141
Candlemas   21, 21
Carbuncle   58
Cell, monastic   21, 22, 36, 64, 66, 71, 72, 76
Chair of Peter, feast   53, 87
Chapter room   14
Cherubim and Seraphim   87
Choir   10, 21, 70, 71, 76, 77, 80
Christ's appearance   12, 36
    as child   22, 30, 32, 36, 50, 72, 74, 75, 79, 102
    at age 3   85
    at age 4   30
    at age 8   50
    at age 18   46, 77
    at age 30   86
    at age 33   50
    Baptism in Jordan   137-138
    Beloved   72
    Betrayal   152
    as Bridegroom   20, 159
    Circumcision   115
    Crib   112
    On cross   79
    Entry into Jerusalem   150
    Face   65, 72
    Father   17
    Finding in Temple   133-135
    Flight into Egypt   126-131
    Footwashing   56
    Light   21

    as Martyr   36, 42, 48, 51, 72, 79
    Mighty king   50
    Miracles   148
    Mother   10, 17, 19, 22, 32, 46, 48, 51, 99, 105, 124, 133, 155
    Name   60, 117
    Nativity   108, 112, 114
    old man   72
    Passion   12
    Presentation   123
    Saints   17, 19
    Scourging 72
    Thorns   72
    Wounds   28, 59, 60, 70, 72, 77, 81, 82
Christendom 82
Christina Ebner   35
Christina of Kornburg   64
Christmas   16, 17, 50, 54, 70, 74
Church   71
Circumcision of Our Lord   70
Communion   5, 20, 155
    received Our Lord   13, 14, 17, 23, 24, 29, 30, 31, 38, 41, 43, 35, 48, 50, 68, 70, 72, 84, 93
Compline   51
Confession 68; general   14
Confessors   52
Conformity to Christ's will   32, 142
Consolation   41, 42
Contrition   70
Corpus Christi   70
Council, monastic   46
Creation   94
Creator   72
Cross   12, 51, 54, 55, 72, 81, 82
Crown   11, 55, 61, 80
Crucifix   54, 59, 71

Cyprian wine   141

Darkness and Starvation   82
Death, everlasting   95
Dedication of Church   39
Deus, Deus meus respice   59
Devil(s)   7, 14, 88, 92
    saying: "You wretch ..."   71
Discipline   5, 52, 69
Dormitory   66

Easter   31, 78
Eberhart Schutz   70
Ecstasy   72
Egypt   51
Elders   32
Elsbet, cousin   79, 80
Elsbet Ortlieb   66
Enraptured   87
Epiphany   118-122
Erlint, Sister   35
Espousal   32
Evil One   50, 71
Evil Spirit   71, 81, 140, 144
Exetatrix   66

Faith, Christian   109
Faithfulness   81
Famine   83
Fasting   82, 139
Father (God)   24, 25, 48, 51, 55, 65
Flowers   42, 62, 88

Fruits   52, 58, 61, 62, 65

Garden   58, 61
Garment of Innocence   25
     symbolism   11, 80
Gaudeamus Mass   87
Gloria in excelsis   50, 55
Gloria Patri   52
Gnadenfruchttopos (Fruits of Grace motif)   8, 10, 11, 13, 14, 18, 19, 31, 32, 36, 38, 39, 45, 48, 50, 55
Godhead   72, 95, 108
Good deeds   11
Good Friday   78, 80
Gospel   32
     John   2, 4, 8, 12, 18
     Luke   1, 2, 4, 7, 22
     Matt.   3, 26
Grace   70, 72, 88
Guardian angel   14, 24

Hackle   52
Hair shirt   69
Harp   14, 88
Heart   62, 55, 95
     exchange of   50
     inscription   15, 25, 32, 33, 45, 45, 117
Heaven   22
Heavenly host   22
Herman Kramer   60
Hohenstein   70
Holiness, mirror of   64
Holy Innocents   125
     feast of   18
Holy Spirit   24, 25, 32, 48, 51, 55, 65, 95, 98, 100, 130, 137, 138, 161

Holy Thursday   8, 56, 72, 76, 154-155
Holy Trinity, feast   26
Hours, canonical   70
Humility   53, 101, 159, 161

I = Adelheid Langmann   1
Illness   71
Indwelling   11, 50, 62
    of Holy Spirit   1
Infirmary   26, 29
Interdict   82

Jerusalem   72
Jesus Christus   60
Jordan River   137
Joseph, saint   126
Jubilation   70
Judgment Day   81, 92, 94, 105
Jutta Pfinzing   92

Kaisheim   70
Kiss   30, 42, 81

Lady's chamber (*kemenate*)   42
Lamb   17
Last Day   25
Laughing   16, 75
    and crying   70
Lent   59, 80
Light   67, 79

Liturgical texts
- *Agnus Dei*   11, 19
- *Ave Maria*   52, 68, 79, 81
- *Beati Dei Genetrix*   84
- *Beati* immaculati   52
- Benedictio *Dei*   53
- *Deus, Deus meus respice*   59
- *Gaudeamus* Mass   87
- *Gloria in excelsis Deo*   50, 55
- *Miserere*   52
- *Pater Noster*   52, 60, 91
- *Requiem aeternum*   52
- *Sequence*   30
- *Te Deum, laudamus*   48, 51, 55
- *Te Deum Patrem ingenitum*   52
- *Veni Creator Spiritus*   10, 52

Lord's Prayer (*See* Pater Noster)   46

Love   11, 94, 95
- drunk with   159
- game of   159
- sickness   72, 119

Low Sunday   52

Marquard Tockler   61
Marriage (*See also* wedding)   19
Martyrdom of Our Lord   1, 48, 51
Martyrs   32, 82
Mary
- beautiful Lady   67
- intercession   48
- Mother   72, 160, 161
- Mother of God   70, 82
- Mother of Mercy   67
- Our Lady   84

Queen   74
Queen of Heaven   70
Womb   103, 106
Mass   16, 17, 18, 19, 25, 29, 30, 32, 33, 43, 44, 50, 51, 59, 70, 84, 86, 156, 157
Matins   66, 75, 76, 80, 92
Meditate   1, 12, 32
Mercy   81, 94, 102, 159
Mildness   81
Miserere   52, 5
Monastery   35, 59, 60, 61, 64, 69, 70
Monk   70

Name, inscribing   15
Nanny (Kunigunde)   67
None, office of   21, 59
Nothing lacking (See perfection)   42, 43, 72, 98
Nuns   21, 59, 67, 70, 71, 82
Nuremberg   61

Obedience   14, 80, 81, 88
Order, Dominican   34
Our Lady (*See* Mary, Mother)   19, 30, 36, 48, 50, 53, 74, 75, 79

Palm Sunday   80
Paris   61
Pater noster   52, 60, 91
Patriarchs & Prophets   52, 55, 82
Pentecost   24, 31
Perfection   32, 35, 48, 55, 98, 148
Pilgrim   68
Prayer, deep   70

Preacher, Father   42, 45
Preaching   1
Preface   30
Priest   30
Prime, office of   53, 54, 89
Prioress   26, 70, 85, 92
Profession (vows)   14
Psalter   19
Purgatory   91
Purity   11, 81
    of heart   80

Refectory   26
    bell   36, 49
    reader   36
Requiem aeternum   52
Revelations of Christ
    "She must be mine"   3
    "At her death I will give her the heavenly kingdom   4
    "I will never leave you."   5
    "See how much I have suffered for you."   7
    "You should grow green like the trees."   9
    "I am your father … brother … bridegroom"   9
    "I shall never separate myself from you"   14
    "I will never abandon you."   14
    "Peace be with you."   15, 30
    "It is my divine heart that is the book of life."   15
    "Greetings from the Highest Lamb."   17
    "I will never be separated from you."   19
    "I have married you by giving you my body   20
    "Just as little as I can ever be separated from my Father."   24, 26
    "You should love no one as much as me."   24
    "You are dearer to me than any other human on earth."   25
    "I love you so much …"   25

"Look into your heart."   25

"Gladly bear suffering for my sake."   25, 38

"Beloved, eat the vegetables for my sake."   27

"My Love, my Tender One, my Spouse …"   32

"You shall be blessed forever."   32

"I want to write my name on your heart …"   33

"My Beloved, your mouth is sweeter than pure honey."   35

"My Beloved …"   36, 37, 38, 41, 42, 43, 63, 65, 72, 76, 81

"Be assured, I will never break my divine faith with you."   37

"You are more dear to me than any human being on earth."   38

"You have received me spiritually no less than my mother conceived me bodily."   41

"Your mouth smells of roses and your body of violets …"   42

"Lean down to my beloved heart and rest there like St. John."   43

"Whenever I draw your soul out from your body into my divinity, then you are sick, but whenever I pour my divinity into you, then you are strong."   44

"See now that I love you."   45

"There will be one will between you and me and those in heaven."   46

"I will not be changed into you, rather you should be changed into me."   50

"So I will give you myself …"   55

"I will press your soul to my divinity …"   55

"I will be yours forever …"   55

"My love, it is necessary for me to wash you all over."   56

"I am here as true God just as I rose from the dead on Easter morning."   57

"I have drawn and pulled your soul into the wild Godhead and into the wilderness of my divinity."   58

"Whoever has any illness should stand before a crucifix and should read the psalm *Deus, Deus meus respice* …"   59

"I will lead my Love into the garden of love …"   62

"I have chosen your heart for me …"   63

"With this man I will let you know how much I love you."   70

"Tell me, what had I done to those who martyred me?"   71

Revelations of Christ (*cont.*)
    "'Greatest sanctuary?' It is my holy Body which is daily consecrated."   76
    "Loving Father, have mercy on the people."   82
    "I am the sun …"   87
    "I will grant everything for which you pray …"   87
    "I will pour my heart into her heart …"   156
    "No one can do anything more dear to me than to pray for sinners"   175

Revelation of God the Father
    "Be at peace, I will free you …"   55
    "I will have mercy on them …"   82

Revelation of the Holy Spirit
    "I will never cease …"   48
    "I will give you all the virtues …"   51
    "I will make you so perfect …"   55

Revelations of others
    "The child certainly belongs in a monastery"   00?
    "God is so merciful …"   79

Saints   48, 52, 55, 81
St. Alexius Day   68
St. Augustine   93
    Order of   61
St. Catherine   32, 48, 82
St. David, King   52, 55
St. Dominic   14, 34, 52
St. John the Evangelist   43, 48, 52, 56, 82
    Day   56, 57
        St. John after Easter, feast   28
St. John the Baptist   48, 52, 55, 82
    Day 50
St. Louis Day   87
St. Margaret   32

St. Mark, Pope, Day   92
St. Mary Magdalene   36, 142
St. Mary of Egypt   93
St.. Matthew Day   92
St. Matthias Day   55, 157
St. Michael Day   92
St. Nicholas   20
St. Paul   45
St. Peter   32, 45, 48, 53, 54, 55, 56, 83
St. Peter, the Preacher of Verona   32, 33
SS. Philip and James   4
St. Stephen   82
    Day   51
St. Thomas the Preacher (Aquinas)   88
St. Ursula, 11,000 virgins   49, 82
Sanctus   17, 25
Satisfaction   81
Scripture   93
Sequence   30
School   23
Sext, office of   54
Shawm   14, 88
Shepherds   114
Shrove Tuesday   52
Sign of the cross   1, 14, 30, 50, 71, 88
Simeon   123, 124
Simon the Hermit   70
Snakes and vipers   32
Solomon, King   65
Son (God)   25, 48, 51, 55
Song of Songs   1, 4
Spes and Caritas   72
Star   119
Sub-prioress   66
Suffering   7, 8, 10, 17, 25, 34, 69, 71, 72, 92, 94, 105, 159

Suicide   60
Summer solstice   35
Sweetness, divine   70, 161
Symbolism garments   11, 80
     crown   11, 80

Te Deum laudamus   48, 51, 55
Te Deum Patrem ingenitum   52
Teacher   23
Tears   17, 52, 64, 116
Temple   65, 72, 134, 135
Temptation   14, 61, 140, 144
Terce, office of   54
Three Kings   118
     Day   19, 32, 70
Tree   9, 65
     symbolism   65, 160
Trinity   25, 48, 73, 76, 82, 89, 92, 156, 160, 161
     feast of   94, 95, 113
Truth   99, 154

Ulrich of Kaisheim   156-162
Union   24

Veni Creaator Spiritus   10, 52
Venia   48, 59, 92
Vespers   15, 21, 22, 37, 44
Virgins   32, 82
Virtue   100
Vision   32, 80
Visitation   104
Vows   5, 14

Wedding   2, 9, 10, 16, 19, 41
    band   20
    mystical   32
Widow   5, 49
Wine, undiluted   21
Wreath   61

Year
    1330   24
    1331   31
    1336   70
    1344   82

www.ingramcontent.com/pod-product-compliance
Lightning Source LLC
LaVergne TN
LVHW041701070526
838199LV00045B/1150